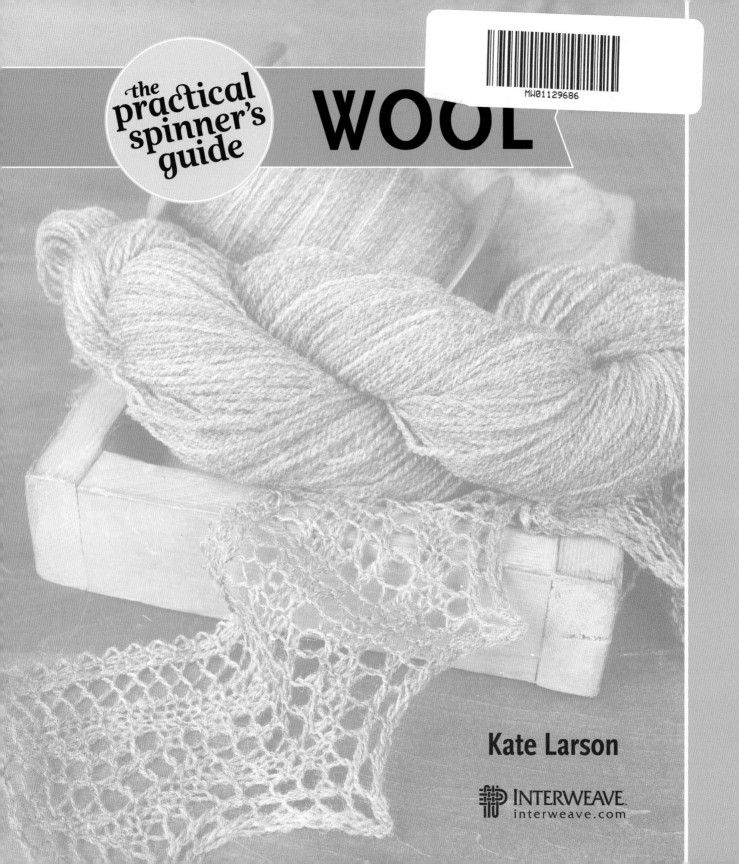

the practical spinner's guide

WOOL

Kate Larson

INTERWEAVE
interweave.com

EDITOR
Michelle Bredeson

TECHNICAL EDITOR
Maggie Casey

ASSOCIATE ART DIRECTOR
Charlene Tiedemann

DESIGNER
Kerry Jackson

ILLUSTRATOR
Kathie Kelleher

PHOTOGRAPHERS
Ann Sabin Swanson, Donald Scott (unless
otherwise noted on page 157)

Interweave
A division of F+W Media, Inc.
4868 Innovation Drive
Fort Collins, CO 80525
interweave.com

Manufactured in China by RR Donnelley Shenzhen.

ISBN 978-1-63250-028-1 (pbk.)
ISBN 978-1-63250-029-8 (PDF)

10 9 8 7 6 5 4 3 2 1

Acknowledgments

THE HEALTHY, VIBRANT handspinning community that I am so lucky to be a part of owes much thanks to Linda Ligon, founder of Interweave, for her vision. A book such as this is brought forth by many hands. Thank you to editor Michelle Bredeson for your kindness and diligent shepherding of this book (and its author); Maggie Casey and Katie Bright for adding further shape and clarity through thoughtful editing; Ann Swanson for her work on the photography and for being in such good humor; and many others at Interweave who added design and form and color to my raw ideas. Through the writing of the manuscript, a number of people offered invaluable help by responding to my research queries and often by reading sections of text. Thank you Elizabeth Johnston, author and fiber artist; Gaby Kienitz, Head Conservator, Indiana State Museum and Historic Sites; Margaret Stove, author and fiber artist; Amanda Hyde, Greenfield Community College professor of biology; Dr. Michael Neary, Purdue University extension sheep specialist; Dr. Ronald Pope, Texas A&M Wool Laboratory; Oliver Henry, Shetland Woolbrokers managing director; the folks at Zeilinger Wool Company; and the many shepherds who contributed their unique perspectives to this project.

I'm forever grateful to the many knowledgeable people I have connected with over the years through a mutual fascination with sheep, wool, and textiles. I'd like to thank W.E. Carter, James Herriot, Wendell Berry, Tim Ackerman, Doug Flack, Susan Markle, Charlotte Dugan, Linda Treat, Amy Clarke Moore, Nancy Bush, Judith MacKenzie, M.L. Ryder, Laurann Gilbertson, and so many more for helping me to forge my woolly path. And, as ever, thank you to my love, my partner in all things, Olaf.

TABLE *of* CONTENTS

Introduction

ON A FRIGID JANUARY MORNING when I was three years old, my father took me to the barn to see a new lamb, born overnight. I vividly remember sitting in the lambing pen in my blue snowsuit, nose to nose with my new friend. As we stared at each other, eager for the experience of first contact, I felt a recognition and a connection that have stayed with me through my life. Sheep are my home.

Many researchers believe that sheep (*Ovis aries*) have been domesticated for about 9,000 years. While discussions about domestication often focus on the impact of human selection upon various animals and plants, this symbiotic relationship in fact runs both ways, causing humans to adapt as well. We have been changed by our relationship with sheep. The process of domestication is more than just taming; it involves imprinting—a rapid form of learning. Imprinting occurs early in life and at critical stages of development, creating associations, behaviors, and even the foundations of identity. Animals and humans are imprinted by one another and the environment in which they live.

We humans have a wonderfully symbiotic relationship with domesticated sheep. We can offer them protection and food, while they can provide us with many of the raw materials we need to survive: meat and milk for nourishment; wool for clothing, blankets, and shelters; horn and bone for tools and ornaments; and an outlet for our deeply human need for creative self-expression. The image that often springs to mind here is of a cozy sweater, but human ingenuity has found an awesome range of uses for wool and other sheep products. Boats fitted with woolen sails allowed people to travel farther and faster in ancient times. Woolen pile carpets from Turkey and medieval woven tapestries from France were highly valued for the warmth and cheer they added to indoor spaces. Fragments of woolen garments and other textiles are found in Viking graveyards. Even sheepskin has been an important sheep product in the past, used to make a variety of things including parchment. The Dead Sea Scrolls and the copies of the Magna Carta still in existence were written on sheepskin parchment that had been carefully stretched, dried, and shaved.

When managed well, sheep can also help us to improve the agricultural spaces we inhabit. Sheep are ruminants, which means they have complex digestive systems that can digest plant matter more efficiently than humans can, allowing them to make use of the landscape in ways that we cannot by converting grasses and woody plants into meat and wool. The valuable manure they leave behind while grazing improves soil, which may later be used to grow crops. Beyond just being a convenient resource, sheep have been partners with humans in creating thriving, diverse agricultural ecosystems.

Handspinning, for me, is a way to explore and savor this connection to the animal and to the land. Even after growing up on a sheep farm and visiting flocks in a number of countries, I have never lost my sense of wonder at the singular relationship that exists between sheep and humans.

Like so many who came before me, I began my life imprinted with the sense of mutual benefit and companionship a life with sheep can afford. Whether you are raising your own flock or learning more about sheep and wool far from any fields or pastures, creating woolen textiles is a link to an important piece of human history. I hope this book shares the spirit of the many far-flung people who feel that a day in which wool is not held in the hands is not complete.

How to Use This Book

In handspinning, as in life, all things are interconnected. This book begins with where wool comes from and an introduction to sheep breeds. You'll also find four pieces I created using my handspun yarns that help to demonstrate the thought processes I go through when spinning yarn for a specific purpose. Sprinkled among the discussions about fleeces and wool science are spinning terms that might be new to you. The glossary at the end of the book can shed some light on any that might be unfamiliar to you.

Chapter One: Wool—Ubiquitous and Enduring

This chapter takes a look at where wool comes from—how it grows, the animals it comes from, and the dedicated folks who produce the wool we love.

Chapter Two: From Raw Fleece to Rolag

Starting with selecting fleeces for handspinning, this chapter covers how to wash and prepare fleeces to create the yarns you want.

Chapter Three: Working with Prepared Fibers

From natural-color rovings to vibrant, textured carded batts, prepared fibers are what many spinners use to create their favorite yarns. This chapter discusses what to look for (and what to avoid) when shopping for spinning fibers. Have you ever wondered what a woolen mill looks like? Take a walk through Zeilinger Wool Company in Michigan.

Chapter Four: Spinning Wool

I offer an introduction to different types of spinning and my yarn design process in this chapter.

Chapter Five: Living with Wool

This section will help you keep your stash of fleeces, fibers, yarns, and textiles organized and safe for years to come.

CHAPTER ONE:

Wool—Ubiquitous and Enduring

1

People spanning the globe have used wool to provide their families and communities with textiles. Looking deeper, we can see that these woolen textiles, the work of our hands, connect us to our environment, our cultural history, and our own personal expression, identity, and evolving aesthetic. More than any other fiber, wool can be used to create a wide variety of fabrics; from dense, hard-wearing Navajo rugs to the fine lace tradition of the Shetland Isles, wool is ever useful and adaptable. Knowing how to make the best use of wool fibers starts with understanding what wool is, how it differs among breeds, and what to look for in a quality fleece.

What Is Wool?

Wool is a beautifully complex protein fiber, composed primarily of keratin. Keratin is a family of fibrous proteins that are part of hard tissues such as hair, feathers, fingernails, hooves, and the outermost layer of skin—all very important in protecting the delicate internal tissues of animals and humans alike. The fiber's outer layer, the cuticle, can be seen under magnification, but can also be felt with your fingertips. The cuticle is composed of overlapping rectangular scales that are arranged like shingles on a roof or scales on a fish. If you slide a lock of wool through your fingertips, it will feel smooth moving in one direction and a bit grabby in the other. And just like your own hair, the grain (texture) of the cuticle is smooth as it moves away from the growth point.

Within the cuticle is the fiber's cortex, which makes up the bulk of the fiber. The cortex is composed of long, narrow cells that give wool a stable crimp. Fine-wool sheep such as Merinos have tight crimp patterns, while longwool sheep have fewer crimps that look more like curly ringlets or a gentle wave. (See pages 17–47 for a discussion of sheep breed groups.)

The cortex can also contain hollow or latticed channels, which are referred to as the medulla. Medullation is found in coarser wools and other types of fibers in sheep fleeces, such as hair and kemp. Hair fibers are smooth and straight and tend to be coarser than wool fibers. Kemp is coarse fiber that is brittle and often shorter than the surrounding wool fibers in a fleece. Both hair and kemp are far less elastic than wool. By comparison, wool fibers are fine and quite elastic, having a natural crimp.

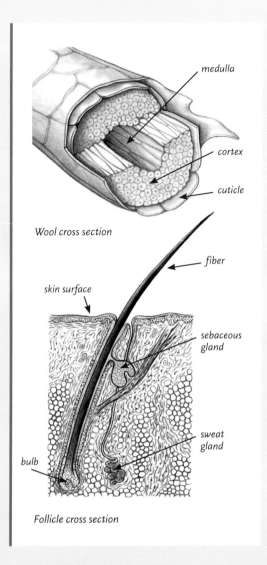

Wool cross section

Follicle cross section

Wool is strong, durable, and elastic, and it has some attributes that make it a fantastic textile material. Wool is a hygroscopic material, which means that it has an affinity for moisture—a handy feature for some textiles, such as woolen socks. And unlike most plant and man-made fibers, wool is flame resistant. It will ignite, but it is self-extinguishing.

Wool Growth

How does wool growth happen? Fibers are created in small tubes set in the surface of the skin called follicles (see illustration on opposite page). As the fibers are formed and journey up through the follicle to the skin surface, the fiber's character is formed.

At the base of the follicle is the bulb. As the fiber begins to form in the bulb and is pushed up through the follicle tube, it is still soft and malleable. Along the way, it begins to harden (keratinize), forming the cuticle. Sebaceous glands that produce wool wax, sometimes called wool grease, lubricate the fibers as they exit the follicle. (Lanolin is one compound found in wool wax, which can be removed from the fleece, refined, and used in cosmetics and lotions.) Sweat glands are also located just under the skin and coat the fiber with suint, a potassium-rich substance that dissolves easily in water.

Measurement Systems

The language used by textile artists, shepherds, and scientists to describe the characteristics of wool can be quite different. To make matters more complicated, terminology and technology come in and out of usage over time, and the same words can be used in different ways in various communities.

Describing the fineness of a fleece (or in other words, the diameter of the individual fibers) is one of the most important ways in which wool can be measured and quantified. There are a number of measurement systems in use, two of which are described here.

Bradford Count

The *Bradford count* takes its name from the city of Bradford in the north of England, a traditionally important wool center. This system of analysis is dependent upon astute wool graders who through practice have learned to categorize wool types by eye and touch. The results are described as the fiber's "quality" or spinning count and are based on how many yards of worsted yarn could be theoretically spun from a pound of combed top. As the wool gets finer, the numbers get higher. The numbers are expressed as how many hanks (skeins), each 560 yards (512 m) long, of singles can be spun from 1 pound (454 g) of top. If a fine fleece is described as 64s, theoretically we could expect 1 pound of this fleece could be spun into 64 hanks, 560 yards each. This system is still in use, but it is gradually being replaced in many communities with micron testing, in which the sizes of the fibers themselves are represented.

Micron Count

Micron count measures the actual diameter of a sample of fibers, the average of which is presumed to be representative of larger lots of wool. Although this sounds very precise, there is still room for interpretation because fiber

Making Sense of Quality Numbers

Interpreting Bradford and micron count numbers can be confusing because they are inversely related. A fine fleece has a higher Bradford count value and a lower micron value. Coarse wools have lower Bradford count values and higher micron values.

diameter is not always uniform throughout the fleece or even throughout the length of an individual fiber. This type of measurement has commonly been used in wool-producing communities in the southern hemisphere for quite some time and is now used alongside Bradford count values elsewhere. A micron is a tiny unit of measurement—one thousandth of a millimeter. The smaller the fiber, the smaller the micron value. A 64s merino is about 21 microns (μ).

The Fine Art of Fleece Selection

Many spinners approach their first fleece purchase with some trepidation. From choosing a quality fleece to washing and preparing fleece for handspinning, there is a lifetime's worth of skills to learn. However, I think it's meaningful to remember that we humans have been at this spinning thing for a while now—spinning wool into yarn is both ancient and modern. Many people in the past have learned these techniques without the aid of books or online videos. This is an art that is as much about trial and error as it is about hallowed tradition. Don't let the idea of ruining a fleece deter you from learning to process your own fleeces. Accidents happen, but they are part of the journey. Wool is a renewable resource: when a sheep is shorn, it is already producing a beautiful fleece for next year. Buying and using wool ensures that shepherds and sheep can continue their important work.

Evaluating and Selecting Fleeces

Evaluating fleeces truly is an art—it's about balancing the many attributes of a fleece and deciding if it is suited to your purpose

A Fleece by Any Other Name

Understanding the language used to describe and quantify the characteristics of wool can be useful. Fiber producers often have a different approach to their product. Remember that many shepherds are not handspinners and may have a way of describing fleece characteristics that differs from the language textile folks use.

or preference. How fleeces are evaluated by commercial wool graders, livestock breeders and judges, and handspinners can be surprisingly different. Spinners typically work fleece by fleece. We don't often need to create large groups of similar fleeces that can be easily processed into consistent lots. This means that spinners might place more importance on how fine a fleece is as opposed to how well it fits a specific breed association's standards, or the natural color of a fleece as opposed to the commercial market's preference for white fleeces.

What should you look for in a fleece? Here are a few of the hallmarks of quality fleeces for handspinners:

Health and Hand

Arguably one of the most important aspects of fleece quality is health, but the specific meaning of health can also be a bit difficult to articulate. Most experienced wool handlers will tell you to be mindful of the smell and hand of a fleece. A healthy fleece should have a mellow, woolly scent. Fleeces that were stored when slightly damp or were from unthrifty sheep with health or nutrition challenges can have sharp, off-putting scents. If you have not spent time working with raw fleeces or sheep, you may need some practice to discern these warning signs. Let experience be your guide.

Hand is also an indicator of fleece health and is as simplistic as it is complex. Hand, or handle, literally refers to how a fleece feels to the touch. Think of it in terms of human hair. Healthy hair feels lively, supple, and sound. Damaged hair feels dry and brittle. Another aspect of the hand when it comes to raw wool is the wool wax, suint, and dirt naturally present in the fleece. How a raw fleece feels when freshly shorn will vary quite a lot by breed, with fine fleeces containing more wool wax than coarse fleeces. Coated and uncoated fleeces will have a difference in hand as well. As handspinners, we are highly tactile people with a sensitive touch. Hand is an intuitive way of describing the many subtle attributes of a fleece we glean through our fingertips.

Character

Character is a broad term encompassing the crimp, color, and luster of a fleece. Handspinners tend to gravitate toward crimpy fleeces. Crimp gives woolen textiles life and loft, often described as memory. Luster, the shiny, reflective quality of some types of wool, can make your handspun glow. Luster varies from breed to breed, but it is a characteristic that some shepherds select for in their flocks. Some breeds have a naturally low-luster fleece that is sometimes described as chalky—many Cheviots are described as having chalky fleeces. Lincoln, Teeswater, and Cotswold are a few of the breeds described as luster longwools. These strong fleeces are highly reflective and often look like liquid sunlight. Additionally, breeds such as Bluefaced Leicester are classified as having a demi-lustrous fleece. And don't assume white is white—fleeces can vary from a bit creamy to a dazzling, bright white. Natural-color fleeces are available in a beautiful range of shades, often with bleached tips in uncoated flocks. Staining can occur for a number of reasons and doesn't necessarily mean the fleece is severely damaged.

Grade and Uniformity

Quality and grade are both terms used to describe the relative fineness of a fleece. While some shepherds choose to have their fleeces micron tested to quantify the fineness of their clip, many do not. For some breeds, such as Cormo and Targhee, consistency in fleece

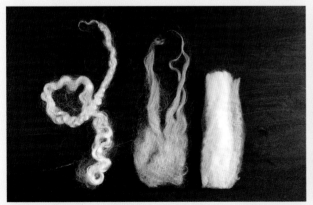

A variety of locks with different characteristics. From left to right: Leicester Longwool, Icelandic, Cormo.

Border Leicester fleece samples showing a change in grade. The locks on the left are from the britch (lower thigh of the back leg), and the curlier, finer locks are from the top of the shoulder.

character from nose to tail is very important. In these breeds, an individual with a fleece that becomes notably coarser in the britch area (lower back leg) would not be considered acceptable for the breed standard. In a Leicester or Lincoln, a britch area that has less crimp, is coarser, and less lustrous than the rest of the fleece is not desirable but is still acceptable.

Staple Length and Strength

The length of fibers produced by a sheep in one year's time will vary from breed to breed. The staple length of the fleeces you are evaluating should be appropriate for the breed. It's not uncommon, though, to find longwool fleeces, which can be up to 14 inches (35.5 cm) long, in the 4- to 6-inch (10–15 cm) range. Longwool shepherds will sometimes shear in nine- or six-month intervals, which makes the fiber easier for a handspinner to manage. In addition to length, it's important to test the soundness of a fleece. Sheep that have experienced physical stress, such as a difficult pregnancy or illness, may have a break (a weak spot) in the staple. You can test for this by pulling an individual lock out of the fleece, grasping it at both ends, and giving a few sharp tugs. If the lock is severely damaged, it may cleanly break in half on the first tug. A lock that does not break completely apart may still produce a crackling sound as some individual fibers sever. A healthy lock will make a distinctive, clear sound, like a ping or a twang.

Purity and Cleanliness

Purity refers to the absence of hair, kemp (short, brittle fibers), and pigmented fibers (in white fleeces). Some breeds, such as Black

Snapping a lock to test strength.

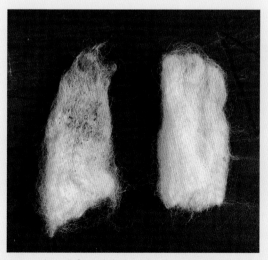

Not-so-clean (left) and clean (right) Dorset locks.

Sheep Coats

Sheep eat forage, and some amount of forage is bound to end up in their fleeces unless most of their body is coated. Sheep coats fit snugly (but not too tightly) from the base of the neck almost to the tail and down the animal's sides.

Romeldale and CVM sheep in coats.

Welsh Mountain, are expected to have some amount of kemp present in the fleece—which is not to say that some breeders won't put hard work into eliminating kemp from these breeds. For handspinners, pigmented fibers in a white fleece are often considered a fleece characteristic rather than a flaw as they would be in a commercial setting. These so-called impurities can in some cases impact dyeing and the hand of a finished textile. Other types of contaminants are acquired by the sheep throughout the production year. Fleeces free of dung, hay, and other barnyard matter are easier to wash and prepare for spinning.

Handling Fleeces: Dos and Don'ts

Handspinners are tactile people—we like to touch everything. When surrounded by fleeces at a competition or sale, it can be difficult to resist laying hands on every bag of wool in sight. While it is typically appropriate to touch fleeces that are for sale, there is an etiquette to handling fleeces that are not yet your very own. Fleeces will have typically been rolled neatly with the shorn side of the fleece exposed. Care is taken to shear and prepare the fleece in one piece, and that careful work is undone if someone grabs a handful of wool and gives a tug. If you're a knitter, imagine someone picking up your lace project and simply pulling the needle out, dropping every stitch. The best way to get a better look at a fleece is to unroll it, but always ask first. If you are visiting a farm, this will be more feasible than if you are shopping at a fiber festival. If it isn't possible to unroll the fleece, try to look inside without disturbing the locks more than necessary. Often, the tips of the locks will be rolled inside the bundle, and you will want to check them for damage and vegetable matter. Additionally, you will want to check the fleece for strength. With permission, pull a small lock from three separate areas of the fleece and check for breaks as described on the previous page (in Staple Length and Strength). Checking in several places will help you know if there is a localized area with tenderness and also allows you to see if the fleece character changes throughout the fleece.

Common Fleece Problems

The types of problems and flaws found in fleeces can be caused by genetics, management, health, and even the habits of particular sheep. Here are a few things to look for when selecting fleeces for handspinning.

Dermatitis—Scurf, Skin Flake, Scale, Dandruff

Dermatitis affects sheep for a variety of reasons, and the impact on the fleece can range from a few tiny, dry flakes that fall out when the lock is teased to a more globby substance that can be a bit gummy and very difficult to remove. This is easier to see in natural-color fleeces but can still go undetected if you are not careful. Dermatitis often affects only part of the animal's body, so if you find a bad patch, keep looking. Scurf is a term often used to refer to the epithelial debris and waxes that make up this white or yellowish matter. Sheep that retain the propensity to shed (i.e., multicoated, or "primitive" breeds) will sometimes have small flakes of skin present in the fleece. As the fibers begin to thin and detach from the surface of the skin, a little dandruff can go along for the ride. (You might see something similar on your own hairbrush.) The shedding process is often aided by a bit of itching and scratching by the sheep, which is technically referred to as pruritus. Scurf, dandruff, and scale are all terms that can

Bluefaced Leicester locks with scurf.

have specific meaning to textile folks, but definitions of and familiarity with these terms can vary widely among researchers, producers, and handspinners in different regions.

Your level of scurf avoidance is a personal matter. For some spinners the "yuck factor" is simply too high, or they feel that their spinning time is too precious to work with imperfect fibers. For others, though, some fleece flaws can be taken in stride and managed (see Intentional Processing, page 90). It's important to note that while dermatitis can indicate a severe health or parasite issue in a flock, it can also indicate genetic propensity, a very wet spring at the farm, mineral deficiency, nonthreatening external parasites— any number of things. So if you find significant scurf in a fleece, contacting the shepherd is a good practice. The cause of the dermatitis might be an ongoing issue, but it could also have been isolated, brief, and undetected.

The specific types of lice and mites that afflict sheep depend greatly upon region and climate. Some parasites feed on blood and can significantly strain the animal's health. Several of these mite species are considered to be eradicated in the United States. Other parasites, like the so-called chewing or biting louse, actually feed on dead layers of skin. While these lice don't impact the sheep's health as significantly, they are more difficult to control. Any parasite that irritates the skin can cause a flaky white matter to be present in the fleece. You will typically find this near the cut end of the locks and most prominently in fleece that grew on the animal's back and upper sides.

Yolk, Stains, and Discolorations

Yolk is an interesting wool-handling term with a long history. It is used by some to describe the mix of suint and wool wax present in any raw fleece, while it is also sometimes used to describe stains and buildup associated with damaged fleeces. A yellow cast to raw fleece can result from climate factors and staining caused by lying in the barn, but it can also have a genetic origin. If you are looking at a raw fleece with yellowed patches or a band of discoloration within the fleece, it could indicate a larger issue—investigate further to see if the fleece has other problems such as scurf or breaks in the lock. In fleeces with a consistent, yellowish cast, most of this color will wash out easily; just give a lock a quick wash in warm water and soap to find out. Any fleece with a significant yellowish color, even if it washes clean, is best washed as soon as possible. The longer the wool wax has to oxidize, the harder it is to remove. If the color indicates a developing bacterial issue, washing will eliminate the problem before the fleece is stored for longer periods of time. Other potential discolorations include pink and green shades that can develop in damp fleeces. Washable spray paint used for animal identification may occasionally be present and is sometimes difficult to remove. Even clay minerals from soil can add a tinge of color to fleeces.

Cotting

Cotting is a term used for felted or matted areas in a fleece. Longwool sheep in particular can cott easily when in full fleece. Typical sites for cotting are the lower neck, from pushing against hay troughs, or the sides, particularly if the animal prefers to lie on one side when resting. It can make processing the fleece for spinning more difficult depending on the degree of damage. Cotting can also be caused by itching, so if you find cotted areas in a fleece, also check for scurf and dander. The matting and felting will often occur midstaple.

Damaged Tips

Fleeces can develop dry, damaged tips as they are exposed to sun and weather. These will feel brittle and often pull off of the lock easily. Also check for milk tips (the tiny curls the lambs are born with) on lamb fleeces as these are especially prone to damage.

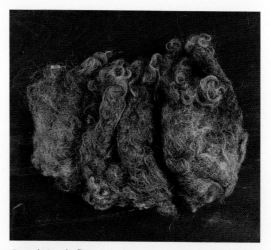

Cotted Lincoln fleece.

Merino-cross locks with damaged tips.

Fleece Contaminants

Sheep eat forage, and some amount of forage is bound to end up in their fleeces unless most of their body is coated. However, a small amount of vegetable matter (VM) in a fleece is not problematic for many spinners, and even a moderate amount of VM is a surmountable problem in many types of fleeces. However, the finer the fleece, the more difficult it can be to remove VM. Burrs and other seeds from sheep that were on pasture can be easier to remove than fine bits of hay chaff. Heavily contaminated areas can be removed with skirting (see page 54), but chaff can also be reduced or eliminated during processing.

Some sheep are genetically predisposed to growing kemp fibers within their fleeces, and sometimes if part of the sheep's face or leg hair was sheared and mixed in the fleece, it can look quite a lot like kemp.

Happy Herbivores

What kind of debris and where it is located in the fleece depends on where the sheep was living. Sheep eating hay at a trough have an interesting habit of jamming in next to their friends, taking a great mouthful of hay and then backing up, dragging the hay across the backs of their compatriots. Hay chaff can also contaminate the fleece on the neck and shoulder from the animals reaching into some types of hay troughs. In these fleeces, removing the center top and sometimes part of the front shoulder during skirting (removing short or very dirty sections of wool) can help. The fleeces of sheep that have been on pasture might contain burrs or other seeds. These are often easy to identify and remove but can prickle fingers.

Beautifully fleeced Icelandic sheep with clean pasture and plenty of space at the feed trough.

Diversity of Breeds

In the next section, we'll look at groups of sheep and the breeds that fall within those groups. But first, let's look at what a breed is.

What Is a Breed?

Breed refers to a specific group of domesticated animals that have similar phenotypes (they look the same). They are also genetically similar, so that offspring produced within the breed look like their parents. However, among purebred flocks, breed characteristics can differ notably in different countries and in different flocks. This is a basic principle of ecology—isolated genetic groups will increasingly differ from each other with the passage of time. The differences we see in, for example, Suffolk sheep in England and Suffolk sheep in the United States, reflect the choices of the shepherds as they select sheep that are fitted to their environment, their farms, and their markets.

The quest for the perfect sheep may lead some shepherds to develop flocks that contain the genetics of several breeds. Many "spinner's flocks" contain crossbred sheep with interesting combinations of characteristics. Somewhere between purebred and crossbred lies the wonderful world of composite breeding: closely managed crossbreeding that aims to combine the best of both parent breeds. This practice brought Corriedales, Columbias, Cormos, and Targhees into production, and they are now treated as distinct breeds in their own rights.

As a shepherd myself, I think it is very important to remember that the genetic composition of a population is never static. A flock is always moving forward—and our choices about what traits we would like to see in our flocks have consequences. Although breeds are groups of similar sheep with a similar ancestry, still they remain fluid over time. This is a good thing.

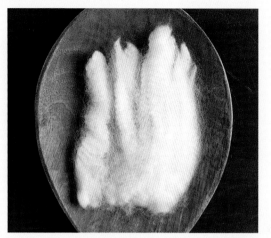

Crossbreeding can combine the characteristics of several breeds. This crossbred fleece unites the fine, dense wool of a Cormo with the curl and luster of a Bluefaced Leicester.

Allowing sheep to adapt to their environment and the needs of the shepherd improves their success and relevance. This should also mean that we are deepening our genetic diversity. Many dedicated sheep breeders are protecting rare breeds, growing their numbers, and keeping their important genes from being lost.

Sheep breeds can be categorized in many ways. It can be truly illuminating to compare how breed lists are grouped in books geared toward livestock producers and toward fiber artists. Lists will also differ depending on the country of publication. The list of sheep breeds you will find here is decidedly fiber-centric. And there are many wonderful breeds not included on this list, but many of the commonly accessible breeds listed here serve as general guides to help you decide what to do with other wools you meet along the way.

How to Use Fleece Statistics

For information on staple length, fleece weight, and micron count, I have researched numerous books, agricultural publications, and breed registries from different countries. The staple length for a breed in the United States might be different than for the same breed from Australia. Generally, I have accounted for these differences by increasing the range included here. Individual flocks may deviate from the range, particularly in flocks where less emphasis has been put on breed standards and more on producing fleeces that the shepherd likes. Even if a flock remains purebred, a shepherd's selection choices can quickly change a flock's characteristics. Fleece size will obviously vary in practice due to the interval between shearings and how much fleece is removed during skirting. The information presented here is primarily helpful in understanding the productivity of a breed in general comparisons. Unless otherwise stated, the staple length and fleece weight will reflect one year's growth from an adult sheep.

Northern European Short-Tail Sheep

The native sheep of the Nordic countries and isles of the North Sea and North Atlantic, such as Shetland, Iceland, and Faeroe, belong to the Northern European short-tail family. As the name implies, these sheep have short, fluke-shaped tails and a common lineage, but they can be quite different in many other respects. Sometimes described as primitive, dual-coated, or multicoated, they have evolved to fit neatly into a variety of environments in northern Europe, including some landscapes in which many other breeds of sheep could not thrive.

Northern European short-tail fibers can be found in a wide range of preparations.

The breeds discussed in this section have all been exported to a number of countries. This adds to the natural variety of fleece types these breeds can provide. Many sheep in the short-tail family have distinctly multicoated fleeces, with long, silky fibers that extend beyond the shorter, finer fibers that grow close to the sheep's skin. Many Shetland and Finn sheep, however, may not show a strong variation within the fleece. Keep this in mind when looking at fleeces or prepared fibers—"Shetland wool" can mean many things!

When selecting fleeces, watch for matted areas. Felting will often occur along the sheep's spine and can be easily removed during skirting. However, some sheep that have a tendency to shed their fleeces can develop large matted areas. Most spinners avoid these fleeces if they have become very felted.

Handspinner's Notes

Prepared fibers from these breeds are often available from shepherds and your local fiber shop. Both Shetland and Finn are available as carded roving and combed tops, but prepared Icelandic is most often found in carded roving form. These fibers typically come in a wide range of natural colors, and the hand can vary greatly.

When starting from fleece, the biggest decision to be made with multicoated fleece types is whether or not to separate the longer and shorter fibers. If separated, each fiber type may be used to its best advantage. For example, the longer fibers could be pulled or combed from each lock and spun into a shiny, firm, worsted warp yarn, while the downy short fibers could be spun into an airy, woolen weft. More typically, spinners leave the fibers together because separating the fibers takes time and produces smaller amounts of fiber.

You can see the range of yarns possible from Northern European short-tail fleeces.

Traditionally, these fleeces were used to create a wide range of textiles and prepared in a variety of ways—think fine knitted lace and cozy long underwear, ship sails and fishing nets. Experiment with woolen and worsted yarns and see what sings to your soul.

Icelandic

FLEECE WEIGHT: 4–7 lbs (1.8–3.2 kg)

STAPLE LENGTH: outercoat: 4–16 inches (10.2–40.6 cm); undercoat: 2–4 inches (5.1–10.2 cm)

FIBER DIAMETER: outercoat: 27–30 microns; undercoat: 19–22 microns

The Icelandic sheep we see today were vital to the settlement of the island nation that gives them their name. As Norse settlers began building communities in the beautiful, rugged terrain of Iceland more than a thousand years ago, sheep provided food, textiles, tools, and even manure to be used as fuel. In present-day Iceland, sheep are still an important fixture in the landscape and continue to provide distinctive meat, milk, and wool products.

In the mid-1980s, Stefania Sveinbjarnardottir-Dignum and Ray Dignum imported the first Icelandic sheep into Canada. From there, Icelandic flocks were also established in the United States. Stefania passed away in 2007, but she is still honored for her contributions to Icelandic sheep in North America and for helping new breeders understand the history and genetics of these special sheep.

Icelandic sheep are known for their distinct multicoated fleeces, with locks containing both long, silky fibers (called *tog*) and shorter fibers (called *thel*), which can be incredibly soft. They come in a variety of markings and color combinations including white, brown, gray, black, and gorgeous mixtures of shades. They have faces and legs clean of wool, and both males and females can have horns. One of their unique characteristics is that they do not have the same flocking instincts as other breeds of sheep. Flock is not only the name for a group of sheep but also a term for the way sheep gather in a pasture and move as a group. Sheep in Iceland roam over the island landscape during the summer. They can forage for food more effectively if they scatter rather than flock together, a habit that they typically retain today.

Icelandic locks.

Icelandic sheep.

Keep Reading

To learn more about the ancient sheep and textiles of Iceland and Greenland, check out *Woven into the Earth: Textiles from Norse Greenland*, by Else Østergård.

Icelandic breeders: Chip and Paulette Brown

Colbert, Georgia • facebook.com/FiddleheadHollow

Chip and Paulette Brown had been raising a wide variety of livestock on their farm, located just outside of Athens, Georgia, when they added a starter flock of Icelandic sheep in 2012. The couple knew that they wanted to produce both fiber and sheep cheese—Icelandics were a great fit. "We fell in love with the breed for their gentility and loving nature." The couple purchased a foundation flock of twenty-two Icelandics after helping with lambing season on a farm in Minnesota.

The flock now has almost fifty head and is quickly growing, with ewes that average two or three lambs each year. Chip and Paulette continue to select for strong milk and fiber production, taking a balanced approach that is in keeping with the tradition of the Icelandic breed. After two years, the Browns are happy with their choice. "We love Icelandics and are thrilled to be on an adventure with them!"

Shetland

FLEECE WEIGHT: 2–5 lbs (0.9–2.3 kg)

STAPLE LENGTH: 2½–6 inches (6.4–15.2 cm)

FIBER DIAMETER: 20–35 microns generally, but fleeces may fall outside of this range

Sheep have played an important role in the Shetland Isles of Scotland for thousands of years. Archaeological evidence shows that by the European Iron Age, sheep's wool was valued for textile use, but researchers believe that sheep were present on the islands long before that. However, much of their history is difficult to trace. Even in recent centuries, these sheep have been shaped not only by the Shetland landscape but also by the need for different types of textiles used over time and by occasional infusions of other breeds of sheep. For a fairly small landmass (less than half the size of the state of Rhode Island), Shetland has varied terrain and a complex geology, making a variety of types of sheep possible. Sheep grazing the rocky areas exposed to the raw coastal weather must be hardy if they are not only to survive but also produce offspring without additional shelter and feed. In areas that are better protected from the elements and where supplemental feed might be provided at times, sheep with less hardy fleece can be reared.

Shetland sheep are quite small, but frame size can vary. They are light-boned and agile, with small ears and eager eyes. Ewes are usually hornless, while rams have rounded horns that spiral as they grow. As flocks of Shetland sheep have been established elsewhere in the world, new environments and shepherding choices have led to further changes in fleece and body type within some flocks and communities of breeders.

For handspinners, the Shetland breed provides a wide range of fleece qualities to choose from.

Fleeces not only vary from animal to animal in color and character but can also differ substantially from nose to tail in the same fleece. In this diversity, we can find fibers for nearly any type of textile we might desire—from incredibly fine fleece for delicate knitted lace to coarser, stronger fleeces for weaving—and everything in between. One thing is for sure, Shetland sheep fleeces from Shetland have a unique hand. Even coarse fleeces feel lithe and full of sea breezes.

Keep Reading

To learn more about the history of Shetland sheep and textiles, check out *Shetland Textiles: 800 BC to the Present,* edited by Sarah Laurenson.

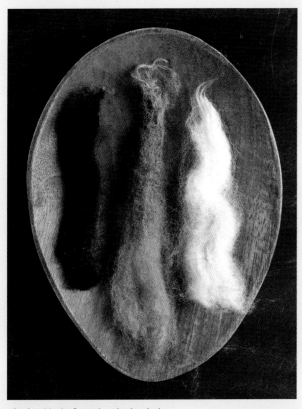

Shetland locks from the Shetland Isles.

Shetland specialist: Elizabeth Johnston, Shetland Handspun

Scousburgh, Shetland · shetlandhandspun.com

Shetland textile artist Elizabeth Johnston uses local wool to spin, knit, and weave traditional garments in her studio on the Shetland mainland. Elizabeth and other textile researchers have made important contributions to the modern use and understanding of the warp-weighted loom, an ancient weaving technology used to create many of the oldest textiles from the Nordic region that survive today.

Elizabeth Johnston shares this about the sheep so ever-present in her life: "Shetland is my fleece of choice; it is an easy fleece to spin, an open fleece, soft, with a loose oil which aids spinning and washes out easily. There are many qualities within the breed and often in one fleece. Close your eyes and touch to feel the softness.

"Spread out the fleece, check for crimp; generally, the more crimp the finer the fiber. See how the 'look' of the fleece changes from one part to the next; that gives a guide to different qualities.

"High-crimp fleece from the neck area is ideal for lace yarn; a looser crimp is needed for yarn for a sweater; the heavier fiber from the back end of the fleece, often with no crimp, is good for a jacket or rug wool but will still have a soft handle. And the variety of color is endless."

Finnsheep (Finnish Landrace)

FLEECE WEIGHT: 4–8 lbs (1.8–3.6 kg)

STAPLE LENGTH: 3–6 inches (7.6–15.2 cm)

FIBER DIAMETER: 22–31 microns

Finland's famous sheep have a long history and, beginning in the 1960s, have been exported to over forty countries around the world. Referred to as Finnish Landrace, Finnsheep, or simply Finn, these unique sheep are often best known for their fine fleeces and fertility. They can conceive at an early age and give birth to litters of lambs—quintuplets are not unusual in many flocks. These light-boned sheep are often described as quite gregarious and friendly, as well as being adaptable to different climates and rough forages.

Finnsheep wool is fine and silky, a longtime favorite of handspinners. Fleece characteristics can range from a tight, organized crimp pattern to a crimp that is less distinct in the lock yet remains bouncy and full. A member of the Northern European short-tail family, Finnsheep can be more or less multicoated. Many fleeces will behave like a single-coated fiber, with each lock containing fibers that are, for spinning purposes, similar in length and crimp character. To check variation in a fleece, pull a few of the longest fibers out of the tip of a lock and pull a few fibers out of the cut end of a lock—lay these side by side and see if you notice differences in the fibers. Finnsheep breeders often have fleeces and rovings available in natural shades—white, brown, and black. Combed top preparations are also on the market and can be spun into yarns that are next-to-skin soft with plenty of loft and durability.

Finnsheep lock.

Finnsheep breeder: Linda Witt, Misty Mountain Farm

Amissville, Virginia • mistymountainfarm.com

Linda Witt, a longtime vendor at the Maryland Sheep and Wool Festival, has been raising Finnsheep in Virginia for over twenty-five years. The very friendly ewes in her flock produce 5 to 6 inches (12.5–15 cm) of wool and four or five lambs each year. Linda says, "We've experimented with a number of other breeds but have decided we like Finnsheep the best. Their fleeces are soft even in old age, their size and temperament make them very easy to handle, and multiple births are a huge plus."

Finn wool has a silky hand and delicate loft that works well for a wide range of textiles. Linda says, "Finn fleece felts quickly and spins beautifully as well. Also, fleeces are light on grease, so there is much less loss when washing fleeces."

Longwool Sheep

The longwool group includes British breeds that produce lustrous, curly locks that can grow up to 15 inches (38 cm) each year. The group contains quite a range of individual fleece types. Within the Lincoln breed, we are likely to find the longest, coarsest fleeces with large curls. At the other extreme, a Bluefaced Leicester might produce downy soft, tight ringlets that reach only about 3 inches (7.5 cm) in length per year. Other breed differences reveal themselves to the spinner's fingertips. For instance, Teeswater fleeces often have a remarkably supple feel that is not only present in the fleece but also in the hand of yarn and finished fabrics.

There are a few fleece issues to be mindful of when selecting longwool fibers. Longwool sheep can be more prone to external parasites that can irritate the skin, causing scurf. Long, silky locks are also prone to cotting. Longwool sheep can easily create cotting by pushing against hay troughs or one another. These matted areas can be difficult (or nearly impossible) to process.

Because long fleeces are more difficult to keep clean and healthy in some climates, many longwool producers choose to shear in six- or nine-month intervals, rather than once a year. Depending on the breed and age of the sheep, these shorter fleeces are still often 4 or 5 inches (10 to 12.5 cm) long.

Handspinner's Notes

Care must be taken when washing longwools to avoid temperature shocks and agitation that cause felting. However, lower water temperatures can often be used when washing these fibers. I have learned to avoid washing

A selection of yarns spun from fleeces from the longwool group.

longwools with temperatures above 140°F to 150°F (60–65°C), as the extra heat can leave these fibers feeling dryer and less lively. You may find different results with your water and detergent combinations.

Longwool fleeces that have a staple length of about 3 inches (7.5 cm) or more can be made into gorgeous combed tops. The combing process aligns the fibers, untangles any snarls, and can allow some bits of hay or seeds to fall

The Leicester Family

During the late eighteenth century, Leicester sheep tended to be lanky and large-framed. A young farmer named Robert Bakewell (1725–1795), returning to his family home at Dishley Grange in Leicestershire, England, noticed that some of the smaller, more compact sheep could be just as productive as their larger counterparts in less time. He set out to improve his flock, eventually creating a new breed called the Dishley Leicester or New Leicester.

Bakewell crossed (mated) closely related animals to amplify certain traits that he wanted in his flock, such as early maturation, shorter legs, and more compact, robust bodies. Eventually, he became one of the most noteworthy figures in the history of animal husbandry and made his contributions to the field of genetics before Charles Darwin or Gregor Mendel were born.

The Dishley Leicesters caused quite a stir. These fashionable sheep could be found throughout Britain and beyond, occupying the thoughts and letters of modern agriculturalists. George Washington and Thomas Jefferson, both renowned shepherds, indicate in their letters that they followed Bakewell's work.

Engraving of a Leicester sheep from the book Sheep: Their Breeds, Management, and Diseases *(1837) by William Youatt.*

out as the locks are prepared. If you're trying to highlight the natural luster of these fleeces, a combed preparation spun with a worsted draw is a good choice. Locks that are flicked or combed individually can also be spun with a worsted draw to yield a silky, lustrous yarn.

A carded preparation is also an option for longwool fleeces that are shorter than about 3½ to 4 inches (9–10 cm). As the fiber is carded, it can be rolled into rolags for a more orderly preparation, or simply left as cloud. Carded preparations incorporate more air into the yarn, making it lighter weight and adding a bit of bounce. When spun with a worsted or woolen draw, you can add more or less structure to the yarn, but it will always have more halo (fibers that stick out of the yarn creating a slightly fuzzy look) and a bit less luster than if combed.

Tailspun and core-spun techniques also work well for curly, long-staple fleeces. Whether you are spinning the fine ringlets of a Bluefaced Leicester or the elaborate curls of a Lincoln, tailspinning allows the locks to remain somewhat intact in the yarn. This is a perfect technique for well-defined locks that are too perfect to disturb with carding or combing. Simply flick the cut end of the lock open and spin one lock after another onto a core yarn.

Leicester Longwool
(Also called English Leicester)

FLEECE WEIGHT: 11–14 lbs (5.0–6.4 kg)

STAPLE LENGTH: 6–14 inches (15.2–35.6 cm)

FIBER DIAMETER: 32–46 microns

Leicester Longwools, like their famous predecessors the New Leicesters, continue to have a distinctive level back and neck and a fleece of long, curly locks, complete with curly topknot.

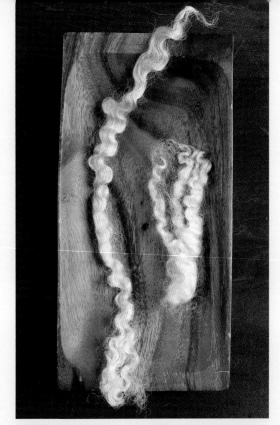

Leicester longwool locks from England. More than one year's growth on the left, six-month's growth on the right.

Leicester longwool sheep on the Glover farm.

Leicester Longwools had all but disappeared in North America by the 1980s but were carefully reintroduced to the United States at Colonial Williamsburg. While new flocks have been established around the country with sheep from the Colonial Williamsburg flock, Leicester Longwools remain on the Livestock Conservancy's critically endangered list in the United States. Leicester Longwools are classed as Vulnerable by the Rare Breeds Survival Trust (RBST) in the United Kingdom and are considered a heritage breed in Australia.

Leicester Longwool breeders: Sonia and Alan Glover, Windy Ridge Flock

Leicestershire, England • windy-ridge.org

Sonia and Alan Glover began their flock of Leicester Longwools in 2007 with ewes from Yorkshire, England. They wisely made their start with ewes that had lambed successfully the previous year purchased from a well-known breeder. They now keep a flock of award-winning Leicester sheep in Leicestershire.

"Our ideal Leicester ewe is tall with good length, well-covered (fit but not fat), weighing 95 to 105 kg. Her wool has high luster and a medium staple with a good crimp. She would have good blue ears and muzzle, and white legs. Why did we get into Leicesters? Just look at them—a picture saves a thousand words, so they say."

Border Leicester

FLEECE WEIGHT: 8–12 lbs (3.6–5.4 kg)

STAPLE LENGTH: 6–10 inches (15.2–25.4 cm)

FIBER DIAMETER: 30–40 microns

During the late eighteenth century, Robert Bakewell's New Leicester rams were crossed with many different native breeds. Some crosses did poorly, while others were so successful they led to the development of several new breeds of sheep. The Border Leicester is widely believed to be the result of crosses of the New Leicester with Cheviot sheep in the north of England and was a well-established breed type by the close of the eighteenth century. Today, Border Leicester is considered a Minority breed in the United Kingdom by the RBST but is found in healthy numbers in both the United States and Australia. Border Leicesters have an elegantly curved head, referred to as a Roman nose, and a sturdy, upright stance. Gentle sheep with intelligent eyes, Border Leicesters tend to be watchful and work easily with their shepherd. Their legs and heads are generally wool free, exposing alert ears that in the United Kingdom are so upright they are often called rabbit ears. They are typically white but can increasingly be found in natural colors. Their fleeces can vary widely from

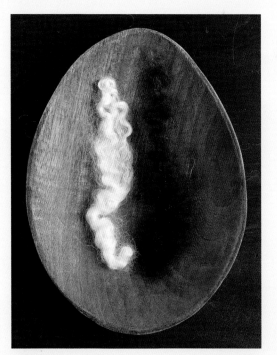

Border Leicester locks.

quite fine and bouncy to strong, bold curls. Locks can be in round ringlets, a flat wave with a purled tip (a gentle curl at the end), and anything in between.

Border Leicester breeders: Ray and Margo Hanson, Marsh Creek Crossing

Twin Valley, Minnesota · marshcreekcrossing.com

Margo and Ray Hanson have a flock of about forty white and natural-color Border Leicesters, not including plenty of bouncing lambs. They got their start when a county extension agent spoke so highly of Border Leicesters that they decided to purchase a small flock for their farm in northern Minnesota.

"I look for the long, lean, and lustrous characteristics promoted by the American Border Leicester Association. I want a ewe that raises a nice set of twins with little help. We live in a cold climate, so a thick fleece with nice curl is desirable for both the sheep and me. A Border Leicester is a dual-purpose sheep, so fast-growing lambs for market with mild-tasting meat are also a plus."

Bluefaced Leicester

(also called BFL, Hexham Leicester)

FLEECE WEIGHT: 2¼–4½ lbs (1.0–2.0 kg)

STAPLE LENGTH: 3–6 inches (7.6–15.2 cm)

FIBER DIAMETER: 24–28 microns

The Bluefaced Leicester is another successful descendent of the New Leicester. The breed was developed in the north of England and was known for creating highly productive offspring when crossed with other types of sheep—a reputation Bluefaced Leicesters still hold today. Of the breeds bearing the name Leicester, Bluefaced is the newest and was a

Border Leicester ewe from the author's flock.

Bluefaced Leicester locks.

28

recognizable breed by 1900. They have dark facial skin under white hair, producing a so-called blue appearance. They often have longer, more tubular bodies than the other Leicesters, upright ears, wool-free heads and legs, and a bowed shape to their heads called a Roman nose. Bluefaced Leicesters exist in healthy numbers in the United Kingdom, where they are crossed with hill sheep to create the highly productive Mule crossbreed, but they are less common in the United States. BFL fleeces are often quite fine with a staple length somewhere between 3 and 6 inches (7.5–15 cm). These fleeces offer such an enticing blend of softness and glossy shine that BFL has become a handspinner's favorite. Most of the BFL fibers spinners come into contact with are processed combed tops, but working from fleeces can be a delight. I often find that BFL locks are more prone to damaged tips than most fibers. Simply remove the tips if they are fragile before carding or combing to dramatically improve your fiber preparation.

Bluefaced Leicester breeders: Tara MacLachlan and Kirsten Tittemore, Little Smoky Blues

Saskatchewan, Canada · littlesmokyblues.ca

Rory and Jody McLean wanted to begin raising Bluefaced Leicesters in Alberta but could not locate any stock in Canada. Together with another Canadian shepherd, they worked to import a flock from the United States in 2007. Their Alberta flock of about twenty was moved to Saskatchewan in 2014. The new owners, Tara and Kirsten, will continue developing the purebred flock and look forward to growing the fiber business. They are also interested in improving the flocks that they had previously: Tara has North Country Cheviots and Kirsten keeps Canadian Arcotts. Tara says she was looking to add a breed that would improve her flock's wool clip and lambing ease

Bluefaced Leicester sheep in Canada.

without losing any of the traits she loves about her North Country Cheviots. She and Kirsten are excited about the future of their purebred flocks and crossbred Mules.

Jody says, "I want a ewe that can keep her weight on. Our winters are harsh, and sheep need good fat cover to keep warm. I like a heavier-boned animal that stands square on her feet. When you put your hand on her back, it should feel like a table top—solid and firm. I also aim for good fleece coverage without compromising fineness. I want at least a 5-pound fleece with good luster and a silky, fine handle."

Teeswater

FLEECE WEIGHT: 7½–15 lbs (3.4–6.8 kg)

STAPLE LENGTH: 6–12 inches (15.2–30.5 cm)

FIBER DIAMETER: 30–36 microns

Like other English longwool sheep breeds, Teeswater sheep were influenced by Robert Bakewell's New Leicesters developed in the late eighteenth century. Taking their name from the Teesdale region in the north of England, Teeswater sheep have white or gray faces with distinctive dark blotches on the face

Teeswater lock.

and legs. Sheep with both white and natural-color fleeces are accepted by some breed registries, while only white fleeces with no dark fibers are accepted by others. Teeswaters have a woolly forelock and long, curled locks that should hang straight without clumping or cotting. They are well known for crossing with other breeds and are used to produce a crossbreed with similar fleece characteristics known as the Masham (pronounced Mass-um).

Teeswater sheep in the United States today are the product of an upgraded breeding method using artificial insemination (often simply referred to as AI). Because sheep cannot be imported from the United Kingdom for breeding purposes at this time, some American breeders have been working to introduce British genetics into their flocks by servicing ewes with imported ram semen. Here's how it works: Ewes from other longwool breeds, such as Cotswold and Lincoln, are selected as foundation ewes and bred to Teeswater rams using AI. If the ewe is a Lincoln, for example, the new lambs are then 50 percent Teeswater, 50 percent Lincoln. Crossbred daughters can then be bred to a Teeswater ram via AI, and the resulting lambs would be 75 percent Teeswater, 25 percent Lincoln. With additional crosses, the percentage of Teeswater genetics continues to increase. The time, expense, and careful management needed to get closer and closer to a purebred American Teeswater is enormous. Dedicated Teeswater breeders on both sides of the Atlantic are working to make it happen.

Teeswater breeder: Susan McFarland, Susan's Fiber Shop

Columbus, Wisconsin · susansfibershop.com

Susan McFarland began raising sheep in 1976 and kept flocks of several different breeds before falling in love with Teeswaters in 2005. She purchased a starter flock of five sheep, some of which were 50 percent Teeswater and some 75 percent Teeswater. Today, she keeps a thriving flock of Teeswaters on her farm in Wisconsin. "When I walk out and see these tall, stately sheep with beautiful black markings, I just can't get over it." Susan's flock now includes a special ewe named Stacie who is 98.99 percent Teeswater. I asked Susan what types of subtle changes she was starting to see in Stacie and other high-percentage Teeswaters, and she said the fleece was far less prone to cotting. "Stacie's fleece has sixteen months' growth right now and looks great. The fleeces of my lower-percentage ewes would have started to become less organized after about twelve months with some fibers beginning to mat and felt."

Lincoln

FLEECE WEIGHT: 11–16 lbs (5.0–7.3 kg)

STAPLE LENGTH: 7–15 inches (17.8–38.1 cm)

FIBER DIAMETER: 34–41 microns

Named for the county of Lincolnshire in the English midlands, these sheep are famous for long, lustrous wool. Until the mid-eighteenth century, Lincoln sheep were tall and rangy, but with the unfolding of the Industrial Revolution, shepherds and livestock improvers began to select for more compact animals that reached market weight more quickly while still producing a full fleece. While considered a rare breed in many places today, Lincoln sheep have been used extensively in many countries to improve other breeds. In some cases, these crosses were so successful that composite breeds were founded, including Corriedale, Columbia, and Polwarth.

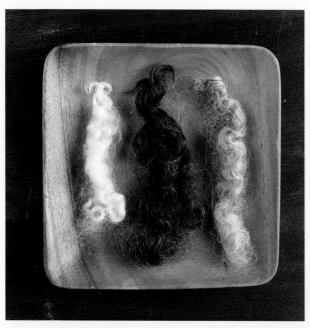

Lincoln locks.

Lincoln sheep have a staid and noble appearance and can be white, charcoal, or black. Even the white-faced, white-wooled Lincolns have distinctive black skin on the nose and often inside their ears. Lincolns are, as a shepherd might say, easy keeping—meaning they are thrifty and can do well on moderate forage. They have heavy, bold curls that extend farther down the leg than on some other longwool breeds. Lincolns are polled (hornless) and have a curly forelock that obscures a gentle eye.

Lincoln breeder: Christiane Payton, North Valley Farm

Yamhill, Oregon • northvalleyfarm.com

"My flock consists of roughly fifty brood ewes as well as stud rams and yearling ewes and rams. Most of the ewes produce twins, some have triplets, and one even had quadruplets several years ago! Because there aren't that many registered Lincolns in the United States, one challenge faced by Lincoln breeders is to keep their gene pool large enough. Most of my sheep trace their lineage back to the more commercially based Lincoln flocks of the Pacific Northwest that existed during the first half of the twentieth century. But we are also fortunate to have introduced genetics from New Zealand and the United Kingdom, as well as from flocks in the American Midwest, so our genetic base is varied.

"Lincolns are best known for their high-luster, long-stapled, wavy, heavy fleeces that have a curl at the end of the staple. These sheep have a hearty constitution and can thrive on a pasture-based diet when many similarly large breeds need concentrates to fuel their growth. And there is no getting around that these are sheep with both brains and personalities; they will steal your tractor keys if you leave it parked in the barnyard. Perhaps bold is the best way to describe Lincolns—a bold fleece, body, and mind."

Down-Type Sheep

Down-type fleeces have a spiral-shaped crimp pattern that is unique, making the fiber difficult to subdue and lending life and loft to our textiles. Down breeds are technically only those that come from the Downs region of southern England. Breeds such as Hampshire, Oxford, and Southdown are true Down breeds. Other breeds with fleeces that will handle in a similar way for our textile uses, such as Cheviot, are often placed in the same category.

Because breeds such as Suffolk, Hampshire, and Southdown tend to have fast growth rates and have become physically large animals in many countries, they are used primarily (if not exclusively) for meat. Where I live in the American Midwest, these breeds are increasingly shown at livestock exhibitions without any wool on their bodies. Even when judging ewes, the wool is removed to show the conformation of the body—the fleece not being considered as important to production. This means that many of the fleeces handspinners are likely to find from these flocks will tend to have more VM, second cuts, etc.

Washing Down-type fleeces is usually quite easy as they typically scour without much work and are slow to felt. Some of these breeds can have a fairly open fleece, and this will vary by country as well as each shepherd's choices. When the wool is less densely placed (fewer wool follicles per inch), more dust and dirt can penetrate deeper into the fleece, closer to the skin. Giving the fleece a good soak in cold water prior to scouring can help to loosen and remove dirt.

Most of the fiber available from these breeds will be raw fleece. However, as more handspinners are interested in spinning Down-type fibers, more prepared fibers are becoming available. Roving and some combed tops are available.

Down-type fleeces can produce a wide variety of yarns.

Handspinner's Notes

Down-type fibers will behave in our yarns just as they behave in the fleece—the fibers don't compress easily. With some types of wool, such as silky Teeswater, even a small amount of twist will squeeze nearly all of the air out of the fiber. Conversely, Down-type fibers, even when prepared and spun into worsted-style yarns, will press against the twist, creating air pockets. This creates loft that will carry through into the finished textile. Some of the breeds tend to produce a fairly short annual staple, so many handspinners card these fibers and spin them into woolen-style yarns. Whether spun woolen or worsted, these bouncy fibers produce yarns that are full, round, and lightweight. Add into the mix that Down-type wools are slow to felt, and we have the perfect sock-knitting wool: full, plump stitches in a lightweight, elastic fabric that is fairly resistant to felting. These bouncy yarns are also great for heavy, cabled sweaters, sweaters knitted in the round without seams, woven blankets, and more.

Cheviot

FLEECE WEIGHT: 5–10 lbs (2.3–4.5 kg)

STAPLE LENGTH: 3–5 inches (7.6–12.7 cm)

FIBER DIAMETER: 27–33 microns

There are a number of different types of Cheviot sheep, but Cheviot flocks around the world can trace their roots back to sheep that lived in the Cheviot Hill region along the border between England and Scotland. These hardy, alert, and productive sheep have done well in many landscapes and have contributed their genes to a number of different breeds. The North Country Cheviot breed developed in the north of Scotland, while the sheep in the Cheviot Hill region became known as Border or South Country Cheviots. Cheviots were firmly established in the United States by the mid-nineteenth century and have continued to change and adapt; many breeders have pushed toward larger, heavier animals, while other breeders have worked to maintain shorter, more compact sheep. The terminology can be confusing: Border Cheviots are often

Cheviot lock.

Cheviot breeder:
Dean Hyden, Shepherd's Bounty
Chewelah, Washington • shepherdsbounty.com

"I have been raising Border Cheviot sheep since 1974. A neighbor to my grandparents was a longtime Cheviot breeder. Mr. Monroe's sheep spoke to my soul and have been a part of my life ever since. I can still trace the lineage of my Cheviot flock back to the very first sheep I received from that shepherd.

"When choosing a look and conformation, I look back to the Cheviots of the 1950s, which I feel had the perfect combination of size and style in the breed. They had a compact body with an upright carriage, tremendous spring of rib, and sound short legs, which gave them the ability to thrive on a grass-based farm.

"The most important aspect of raising any livestock is that you can go out to the barn each morning and are gratified with what you see. Provide clean barns, sound fences, adequate feed, fresh water, and proper minerals, and you will be rewarded with the highest-quality fleece possible."

simply referred to as Cheviots, while there are also U.S. breed associations for Miniature Cheviots, American Classic Cheviots, and North Country Cheviots. While Cheviot character varies, there is a distinctive look to these breeds. Cheviots have small, alert ears that are forward facing, and both males and females are hornless. They do not have wool on heads or legs and also have fairly short necks. And that twinkle in their eye lets you know that they have a reputation for being first-class fence jumpers.

Cheviot fleeces are full and bold but usually feel more crisp than scratchy or harsh. The wool is often described as having a "chalky" look, and fleeces have a matte appearance. I often hear from breeders that some Cheviot sheep can be prone to breaks in the fleece caused by difficult lambing or illness, so check for soundness when shopping for fleeces or carded fibers. Locks often have a more pointed tip than those of traditional Down breeds.

Suffolk

FLEECE WEIGHT: 4–9 lbs (1.8–4.1 kg)

STAPLE LENGTH: 2–4 inches (5.1–10.2 cm)

FIBER DIAMETER: 26–28 microns

Suffolk sheep are easily recognizable for their distinctive black heads that typically have no white wool on the forehead. Suffolks were developed in southeast England, have colored faces and legs, and are hornless. The breed was established in the early 1800s and was being exported to sheep-producing communities outside the United Kingdom by the end of the century. Suffolks are used extensively for crossbreeding and exist in healthy numbers in many countries. As they have been adapted by many different communities, there is some divergence in their appearance. Suffolk sheep in the United States tend to be much taller, and have a longer, smoother body type than they do in the United Kingdom, where they are shorter, stouter, and heavier boned.

Because most Suffolk producers focus on meat, the breed's springy, versatile wool often is overlooked. Fleeces from this very popular breed can be surprisingly difficult to find, and they often have more VM present than we might prefer as handspinners. Staples tend to have a blocky shape and are less distinct in the fleece than for some breeds.

Suffolk lock.

Suffolk breeders: Mike and Lona Bronkema, Shady Side Farm

Holland, Michigan • shadysidefarm.com

Shady Side Farm in western Michigan is a multigenerational, diversified family farm dedicated to sustainability. The farm keeps flocks of Suffolk and Polypay sheep, in addition to other livestock. Farmers Mike and Lona Bronkema started with Suffolks years ago to add more diversity to their farm and to produce lambs for their children to show in 4-H.

Wool quality is not a production trait that many Suffolk breeders in the United States have focused on in recent years. Mike and Lona have selected for fleece characteristics in both of their flocks and sell wool products online and at local markets. Improving the Suffolk flock has been a challenge, though. Mike says, "At one point, we used a U.K. Suffolk ram that helped quite a bit with wool quality and ability to thrive on grass. We would love to use more U.K. Suffolk rams, but they are hard to find here." The different fleece types in the flock are sorted at shearing time and used for different products. Long-staple, higher-quality fleeces are processed into rovings and the farm's famous wool socks. Short-staple and coarser fleeces from the flock are great for bedding products, such as comforters and mattress pads that need to be lightweight and springy.

What do Mike and Lona look for in a great Suffolk ewe? "Our idea of the perfect Suffolk ewe will be one that lambs without assistance and takes care of her lambs. She will have straight legs, a square rear, and a good spring of rib. She will be able to thrive on grass. The health of the sheep is very important to wool quality."

Horned Dorset

FLEECE WEIGHT: 5–8 lbs (2.3–3.6 kg)

STAPLE LENGTH: 2½–4½ inches (6.4–11.4 cm)

FIBER DIAMETER: 26–33 microns

Recognized as one of England's oldest breeds of sheep, Dorset Horn (or Horned Dorset) has long been known for vibrant white wool that is useful for a wide range of textiles. As the sheep age, their horns continue to grow, but at a slower rate. They have pink noses and ears, with a woolly topknot. Some fleeces can be surprisingly fine and lustrous, while at the coarser end of the breed, fleeces are stronger and more robust.

Both males and females have a set of curling horns, and shepherds typically select for horns that curve forward and downward but do not touch the face. While many people love the iconic look of horned sheep, they do come with extra management concerns, such as fencing and feeders that are horn-friendly. Extra care must also be taken with young animals as their horns are more fragile in the first year or so. In the 1950s, efforts to produce a hornless Dorset resulted in what we now call the Polled Dorset breed. (A sheep's poll is the boney

Dorset sheep at Beech Grove Fiberworks.

bump on the top of the head that would have been seated between the horns. Polled sheep and cattle often still have indentations in the head where the horns would have been.) The Polled Dorset has become a very successful commercial breed, while the Horned Dorset exists in smaller numbers and is of conservation concern in the United Kingdom, the United States, Australia, and New Zealand.

Horned Dorset breeder: Bill Carter, Beech Grove Fiberworks

Gaston, Indiana · beechgrovefiberworks.com

Bill Carter began raising Columbia sheep in 1980 but always had an interest in Horned Dorsets, a breed his grandfather raised during the Great Depression. In 2007, Bill and his son, John, purchased their first Horned Dorsets from a farm in Virginia. They were looking for sheep that could do well on grass and could fit into the family's diversified, multigenerational farm in central Indiana. "Our ideal Horned Dorset is a bit more traditional than those currently succeeding in the show ring. We look for a moderate-framed sheep with lots of depth of rib and a balanced conformation that provides an advantage on pasture and a long productive life.

Horned Dorset lock.

"We were very fortunate to find our ideal fleece on the very first Horned Dorset that we purchased. A fleece with a defined crimp structure to be sure, but with a surprising degree of fineness and density, and a buttery soft handle. Our goal is to simply reproduce this fleece throughout our flock."

Medium-Wool Sheep

Medium-wool fleeces play an important role in woolen textile production—they can be soft and fine yet are strong enough to be durable, and they can be supple yet have memory and resilience. Fleece from these breeds can be used for everything from woven blankets to knitted lace. Individual flocks within the breeds listed here can vary greatly, often edging into fine-wool or Down-type categories. Corriedale wool in the United States can range from hardworking, sturdy fleeces that have

rectangular, blocky staples, to deliciously soft, fine fleeces. Medium-wool breeds are dual-purpose, meaning they produce meat as well as wool. However, in many regions economics often pushes flocks toward meat production to the detriment of fleece quality and quantity. Today, the Internet allow shepherds to market fleeces directly to handspinners as never before. These new opportunities have allowed shepherds with small- to medium-size flocks to select for higher-quality wool (which to many means finer wool) and work to keep fleeces cleaner.

In uncoated fleeces, watch for "tippy" (damaged by sun and rain) fleeces, and check for amounts of VM that are in excess of your tolerance.

Handspinner's Notes

Corriedale, Columbia, Tunis, and other breeds that often fall in the medium-wool category range from having a crisp hand to denser staples with an organized crimp that lean more

Several yarns spun from medium-wool fleeces shows the diversity of these fleeces.

toward fine wools. (These generalizations also depend on where you live. Spinners who live in regions where fine-wool production is common will approach wool a bit differently than spinners in areas where longwools or Down flocks are predominant.) All of these wools can be combed easily when the staple length is over about 3 inches (7.5 cm). Combing is a great way to quickly open these locks and to remove debris if you are working with fleece that contains lots of bits of hay. Combed tops from these breeds are often easy to spin and yield a

smooth, durable yarn that highlights any natural sheen the fiber might have. I personally find that the cuticle of these fibers is often quite pronounced. So when spinning combed top or flicked locks, I like to spin with the direction of the cuticle. Try both directions and see what you like. When fleeces are shorter than about 3½ inches (9 cm), carded preparations might put these buoyant wools to best use.

Tunis

FLEECE WEIGHT: 6–15 lbs (2.7–6.8 kg)

STAPLE LENGTH: 3–5 inches (7.6–12.7 cm)

FIBER DIAMETER: 24–30 microns

When North African fat-tailed sheep arrived in the United States, their genetics were introduced into many flocks, creating what we now call the American Tunis (or simply Tunis). These thrifty sheep with distinctive red faces and legs began spreading throughout the United States in the early nineteenth century. The breed was widespread by the 1860s but was nearly eradicated during the Civil War. The numbers of Tunis sheep in the United States have been growing, but the breed remains on the Livestock Conservancy's Watch List.

The American Tunis has become a much larger animal in recent decades, but their distinctive cinnamon-colored heads and legs have remained an important feature. They have white wool after the darker lamb fleece is shorn and have very little wool on the crown of the head. Fleeces from some Tunis sheep can have the crisp, springy feel of a Down breed, while others have a finer, suppler feel, more like other medium-wool sheep. The finer-type Tunis fleeces are soft enough for many people to wear next to the skin. The loft and bounce of this evenly crimped wool is a great choice when spinning for large textiles

Tunis lock.

Tunis sheep and friend.

such as blankets and cabled sweaters that also need to feel fairly soft in sensitive hands.

Tunis breeder: Kim Day, Red Rope Farm

Douglassville, Pennsylvania · redropefarm.wordpress.com

Fiber artist and farmer Kim Day first encountered Tunis sheep at a county fair when she and her husband were living in northeast Philadelphia. After moving to a farm in 2004, they visited several sheep producers, trying to decide what breed of sheep they wanted to raise. "We started leaning toward Bluefaced Leicesters, but something about those Tunis sheep from the fair kept tugging at us. They were so beautiful and didn't look like other breeds with those red heads. Plus they were so gentle—totally content to lie in the straw while I stroked their heads and faces. We ended up purchasing our ewes from the same family whose sheep we saw at the fair."

The Days keep a flock of about a dozen Tunis sheep in their lively Pennsylvania barnyard. Kim sells raw fleeces but also has her Tunis clip processed into rovings and millspun yarns. She looks for "clean, soft fleeces that have a generous staple length (preferably 3½ inches [9 cm] or longer), and good crimp."

What does Kim look for in a Tunis ewe? "My focus for breeding is keeping the traditional look of Tunis sheep. Therefore, I want my sheep to be of medium height and well muscled, have a docile temperament, good mothering instincts, and beautiful wool."

Columbia

FLEECE WEIGHT: 10–16 lbs (4.5–7.3 kg)

STAPLE LENGTH: 3½–6 inches (8.9–15.2 cm)

FIBER DIAMETER: 23–31 microns

Columbia is an American breed developed to suit the rangelands of the western states, but flocks can now be found in many parts of the country. United States Department of Agriculture research that led to the dual-purpose Columbias we see today began in the early twentieth century and was founded on a Lincoln-Rambouillet cross. Many flocks have been selected for frame size and are some of the tallest sheep you are likely to meet, while other flocks maintain a more moderate frame. They have smooth, clean faces and large pink ears covered in white hair that are often described as pendulous because they do not stand upright. Columbia fleeces vary in fineness and crimp character to some degree and are typically quite large. The bold, blocky staples can look quite similar to those of other breeds, but Columbia wool has an extra spring and vigor to the crimp profile. There is an added crispness that makes this fleece an excellent choice for textiles that will be heavily used but still need to be inviting to the touch. Handspun, handknitted Columbia socks are durable and lively, making them as enjoyable to wear as they are to make.

Columbia lock.

Columbia breeders: Gene and Mary Langhus, Langhus Sheep

Big Timber, Montana • langhussheep.com

The Langhus family first introduced sheep onto their farm in south central Montana in the late 1980s to help control leafy spurge (*Euphorbia esula* L.), an invasive plant species that was growing on their property along the Boulder River. Over twenty-five years later, they have a nationally respected flock of about seventy-five Columbia ewes. Gene, Mary, and their children have carefully managed the flock, using statistical analysis to help them select for highly productive sheep. Since 1991, they have participated in the National Sheep Improvement Program (NSIP), a nonprofit organization that helps shepherds take a scientific approach to management by compiling performance data such as wool and carcass quality and growth rates. Mary says that "extensive farm records and the NSIP tools have assisted us in identifying and selecting superior breeding stock for economically important traits."

What do Gene and Mary look for in their Columbia ewes? "Our ideal sheep would exhibit excellent maternal, growth, carcass, and wool traits. We would like for ewes to have a single lamb at one year of age, and raise twins for at least the next eight years. The lambs should gain well and weigh 60 pounds or more at 60 days of age and 120 pounds or more at 120 days of age. We like fleeces to be uniform in fiber diameter and crimp from shoulder to britch, with a distinct crimp formation, longer staple length, bright white color, higher volume of clean wool (less lanolin), and a soft handle."

Corriedale

FLEECE WEIGHT: 10–15 lbs (4.5–6.8 kg)

STAPLE LENGTH: 3–6 inches (7.6–15.2 cm)

FIBER DIAMETER: 26–33 microns

When Merino sheep from Australia were established in large numbers in New Zealand in the 1840s, it didn't take very long for them to become a permanent fixture in the diverse New Zealand landscape. Sheep farms and pastures were established throughout the islands within a few decades, and breeds such as Lincoln, Leicester, and Romney were added to the mix. Crosses between the British breeds and Merino were used to create sheep that were highly productive and adapted to the climate. James Little, the manager of a New Zealand estate called Corriedale during the late nineteenth century, is remembered for his work in developing a Longwool/Merino cross that would become the Corriedale breed.

These successful sheep exist today in healthy numbers in many parts of the world. As they have been adapted for different environments and purposes, they have become quite a diverse group. They can be white or natural colored, have wooled legs and foreheads, and range from quite large with long legs and necks to shorter, more sturdily built sheep suited to grazing, with many types in between.

Corriedale breeder: Geof Ruppert, Ruppert's Corriedales and Windborne Farm

Fairfield, Pennsylvania • ruppertscorriedales.com

The World Corriedale Congress brings shepherds together from around the world to share their perspectives and goals for this popular sheep breed, which can differ widely around the world. Geof Ruppert, a Corriedale

Corriedale lock from the Ruppert flock.

producer from Pennsylvania, attended the event when it was held in Ohio in 2000 and was inspired by sheep breeders from Australia and New Zealand to make changes in his flock. He had a chance to see fleeces coming from the southern hemisphere that were much finer, more lustrous, and longer stapled than fleeces that were trending in the United States at the time. In the next few years, Geof began introducing Corriedale genetics from Tasmanian and Victorian flocks in Australia into his Pennsylvania flock through artificial insemination. He says that he wanted to "go back to the roots of the breed and bring Corriedale wool back to the Corriedale." After introducing new genetics and refining his flock over the last twelve years, Geof now sees his ideal ewe as "medium sized, correct on feet and legs, with a generous wool cap over an open face, and wool down all four legs. Fleeces should be lustrous and fine from end to end, with a bold crimp."

Fine-Wool Sheep

The quest for the most luxurious wool and the softest cloth possible has been with us since ancient times. And the finest wool comes from one of the world's most notable breeds—the Merino. Today, Merino is a family of breeds that can produce different types of fleeces in a wide range of environments around the globe. Merinos have also been crossed with other breeds, giving us many interesting composite breeds, such as Cormo and Polwarth, which can create flocks that are better adapted to their environment and the needs of the shepherd.

Fine-wool fleeces are more commercially viable than those of other breeds loved by handspinners. Much of the marketability of fine wool is based on consistency and quantity. Many Merino flocks have finely honed genetics. Their wool is tested and selected for fiber diameter and consistency so that fleeces can be grouped into large, reliable lots and sold to the textile industry. This means that even fine-wool sheep raised in smaller flocks that provide fleeces for handspinners will typically have fleeces that have a very consistent fiber diameter and crimp from one end of the sheep to the other.

Merino, Rambouillet, and Cormo fleeces can be quite large, containing a huge amount of wool. When fleece shopping, watch for breaks in the fleece and damaged tips. These weak spots can break easily during processing and cause neps and noils.

Handspinner's Notes

Merino, Polwarth, and other fine wools are readily available as combed top. During combing, all of the short fibers, damaged tips, and VM are removed, leaving only perfect fibers. Dyeing can be done prior to the final combing or after the fibers have been combed.

Fine-wool sheep produce fleeces that can be spun into an endless variety of yarns.

Fine fleeces can also be purchased as carded rovings; however, fine wool is more easily damaged by carding machines, creating neps and noils that will be in the final roving. This can make spinning fine, even singles far more difficult. Additionally, second cuts, VM, and scurf that have been carded into the fleece are difficult to remove.

Fleeces in the fine-wool group can range from moderately fine with lots of body and personality to supple, downy-soft, and superfine. When carefully carded to avoid breakage, these fibers can be spun into airy woolen yarns that have a beautiful matte halo. When combed, the smooth worsted yarn that results can be knitted, crocheted, or woven into fabric with great definition and clearly visible patterns.

Romeldale and CVM

FLEECE WEIGHT: 6–15 lbs (2.7–6.8 kg)

STAPLE LENGTH: 3–6 inches (7.6–15.2 cm)

FIBER DIAMETER: 21–25 microns

In the early 1900s, A. T. Spencer, a California sheep producer, purchased New Zealand Romney rams to breed to his Rambouillet ewes, eventually resulting in the Romeldale breed. Today, Romeldales can be white or natural colored but are less variegated than their cousins, the California Variegated Mutants. CVMs, as they are often called, were developed in the 1960s when natural-colored lambs with badger face markings were born in the Stone Valley Ranch flock of white Romeldales in California. Glen Eidman, a shepherd working with the Stone Valley Romeldales, started a small flock based on the natural-color sheep. He continued to select for color and fleece quality until he developed the CVM breed, which is identified by its interesting color patterns and shifting shades in individual fleeces. Interestingly, the beautiful colors found in these fleeces darken as the animal matures, unlike most other breeds that lighten as they age. These fine-wool sheep are now found in many parts of the United States but are considered a critically endangered breed.

Romeldales can be either white or natural colored. What differentiates a CVM from a natural-color Romeldale is varigation. Classic CVM markings are a distinct light-colored stripe that extends from nose to eyes, referred to as a badger face, and a light-colored body with a darker belly.

Romeldale/CVM lock.

Romeldale/CVM sheep.

CVM breeders: Yvonne and Doug Madsen, Spinners Eden Farm

Bellingham, Washington • spinnersedenfarm.com

Yvonne Madsen had been spinning for a number of years when she found a beautiful, mottled-gray CVM fleece for sale that had her name on it—the fleece was from a sheep named Yvonne! She had it processed into roving and remembers that it was "soft, fluffy, and a different texture than I had ever spun before. I fell in love with it!" In 2007, Yvonne and her husband, Doug, moved to a farm outside of Bellingham, Washington, and began their Romeldale/CVM flock. Today, their flock of about thirty includes an array of solid and variegated colors.

"The ideal sheep in our flock has fine, soft, crimpy wool with staple length about 4 inches (10 cm), shearing about once a year. The sheep are all coated and require several changes of size as their wool grows—most of our sheep cooperate with this plan. We like sheep with good dispositions and are very hands-on with our small flock. We love all colors. There are several alleles involved in the color genetics, so the day the lambs are born, it's a little like Christmas, with lots of color surprises."

Cormo

FLEECE WEIGHT: 5–12 lbs (2.3–5.4 kg)

STAPLE LENGTH: 3½–5½ inches (8.9–14.0 cm)

FIBER DIAMETER: 21–23 microns, but some fleeces may be as fine as 17 microns

While the origins of some breeds are nearly lost to the mists of time, more recent additions to the world's sheep breeds have clear and recorded histories. The Cormo breed was developed starting in 1959 at Dungrove, a sheep station near Boswell, Tasmania. Ian

Downie and his wife, Anne, were raising superfine Saxon Merinos and wanted to make some changes in the flock to create sheep that were more productive on the Dungrove property in the Central Highlands. With the help of a genetics research group in New South Wales, Australia, Downie developed a breeding program where Corriedales were crossed with his Merinos. He gathered data on fleece weights and impurities, twinning rates, and body size. This data was then used to make informed decisions and eventually the Cormo (named for both breeds—Corriedale and Merino) was developed. The Downie family continues to develop the Cormo sheep on the Dungrove property to live in better symbiosis with the Tasmanian landscape. Cormos have been exported to a number of other countries, including the United States, where they are now adapting to new environments.

Cormos are known for producing dense, consistent fleeces. The wool is typically a beautiful bright white and is 21 to 23 microns in diameter. These long, fine fleeces are well stapled and make stunning worsted-spun yarns when combed. Spinners often report that Cormo fleeces can be a bit more difficult to prepare without creating neps and noils than other fine-wool fleeces. Gentle preparation is key and well worth the time and care—handspun Cormo yarns are a joy to use and wear.

Cormo breeder: Sandra Schrader, Clear View Farm

Waterman, Illinois · clearviewcormo.com

Sandra Schrader raises a flock of about twenty Cormos, which she started in 2005. She is a great advocate for the breed and is active in the American Cormo Sheep Association. The distinctive, velvety wool of the Cormos are important to her, but she likes to take a balanced approach to selection.

Cormo lock.

"When Ian Downie created the Cormo breed, he not only wanted quality wool but he also wanted hardy, high-producing, fertile flocks. His primary motivation for developing this breed was to increase the economic value of his flock. By maintaining a balanced approach to breeding, a shepherd can make sensible decisions to maintain all the important traits of the Cormo breed in the future.

"When I look for my ideal brood ewe, I look for uniform crimp, staple lengths of 4 to 5 inches (10–12.5 cm), and a fiber diameter of 18 to 20 microns. Physically, she must have a level back, standing square on all legs, and have a deep body capacity. Our brood ewes should lamb with minimal assistance. They should be good mothers, caring for all lambs they produce, providing ample milk. I have high expectations!"

Merino

FLEECE WEIGHT: 7–14 lbs (3.2–6.4 kg)

STAPLE LENGTH: 2½–5 inches (6.4–12.7 cm)

FIBER DIAMETER: 18–24 microns generally, but can be finer and coarser

The fine-fleeced Merino sheep developed in Spain have influenced wool production around the globe as we have pushed for ever-softer, luxurious cloth. During the Middle Ages, Spain guarded its fine-wool flocks, and it was illegal for these lucrative sheep to be exported outside of the country. But in 1723, the Spanish royal court sent a flock of Merinos to Sweden, and within a century, additional flocks were established in many countries around the world. As the sheep adapted to their new homes, new strains of Merinos were developed, adding additional branches to the Merino family tree. Merino types are differentiated by how well they are adapted to different environments (relatively dry or damp) and fleece character (staple length, fiber diameter, color, etc.). Modern Merino strains and breeds include Saxon, Peppin, Tasmanian, Delaine, Est à Laine, and Rambouillet.

The vast majority of Merino sheep the world over are white, but natural-color flocks exist in shades of taupe to tan to chocolate brown. One of most important aspects of Merino fleece is that the wool follicles are very closely placed. Merinos can produce dense, firm staples of incredibly fine fleece with regular crimp. Merino fleeces are also described as high in grease, losing an average of 50 percent of their weight during scouring. Washing these fine fleeces without causing felting can be a challenge, but the result is fine wool that is so divine, it has captured our interest for hundreds of years.

Keep Reading

To learn more about the history of the Merino breed and the process of working with very fine wools, check out Margaret Stove's book, *Merino: Handspinning, Dyeing, and Working with Merino and Superfine Wools.*

Merino breeder: Sally Fox, Viriditas Farm and Foxfibre Cotton

Brooks, California · vreseis.com

Sally Fox loves natural color. She is internationally recognized for her work in developing modern, organic, natural-color cotton genetics—and she also raises sheep. Her flock of about ninety superfine Merinos plays an important part in building healthy soils on Sally's farm in California's Capay Valley, where the sheep are rotated with cotton, heirloom wheat, and milo. Sheep graze rangeland hills and cropland after harvest (often called stubble), keeping invasive weeds in check while producing valuable fertilizer—manure. The manure the

Merino locks.

Merino sheep in Sally Fox's organic pastures..

sheep leave behind increases soil organic matter, which feeds soil microbes, leading to improved water-holding capacity and rainwater infiltration rate. As the sheep have done their important work over the years, Sally has watched for changes in the landscape. "On the hillside, organic matter is being added, and topsoil is actually being formed—it's absolutely amazing and wonderful. The goal is to have more than ten species of plants in a square meter."

Already a longtime entomologist and cotton breeder, Sally also had a growing interest in biodynamic farming that led her to add the Merino flock in 2000. Biodynamic farmers believe that animals play an integral role in the health of the landscape. When Sally heard about a flock of certified organic, natural-color superfine Merinos that was for sale, she intended to purchase six. Instead, she came home with a flock of thirty ewes that would, unbeknownst to Sally, begin lambing in a few

days. Despite a rough start, the flock has continued to grow. Sally selects for ewes that thrive in her landscape and have good mothering instincts and calm dispositions. She is increasingly focused on fleeces and is working to broaden her color range and increase the staple length of her already fine fleeces.

Working with Wool:

Unst Jumper

Unst is a beautiful, windswept island in the North Sea. Located in the Shetland Isles, off the northeast coast of Scotland, Unst is the northernmost inhabited place in the British Isles. Due to a unique geology, the varied landscape yields a wealth of rocks in a palette of colors that seems to echo the natural color fleeces of the native sheep. The handspinners of Unst were well known in Shetland for their skill in spinning fine lace yarns.

Shetland's beloved sheep have a wide variety of fleece types, markings, and physical characteristics. I wanted to create a textile that combined different Shetland sheep fleeces I have gathered in the United States as well as Shetland. Each color is from a different farm and has quite different characteristics. When spun similarly and fulled a bit before knitting, they fit together quite nicely into a jumper.

Unst, Shetland Isles.

Spinning

While a carded preparation and woolen-spun yarn are now commonly used for Shetland and Fair Isle stranded knitting, worsted yarns were also used. Knitted pieces in the textile collections at the Shetland Museum and Archives in Lerwick are made up of a wide variety of yarns. Considering the types of fleeces I would be working with for my jumper, I decided to card the fleeces into a woolen preparation and spin them with a woolen long draw.

Sampling for this type of project is important. When working with natural-color wool in particular, you will find that there may be striking differences in wool character from color to color. Spin and wash small samples of each color before jumping into the entire project to be sure that the finished yarn gauge of each color is similar. I chose to spin a soft, airy fingering-weight yarn using five natural colors. I spun the yarns so that they had a bit of extra ply twist. I finished the yarns with slight fulling to settle the extra ply twist and to add durability. Because the fleeces I used had different wool characteristics from one to the next, I wanted to finish the yarns before knitting so they would not change dramatically after I knitted them.

Knitting

I wanted to create a very lightweight, fine-gauge garment, so I used a traditional construction that didn't create heavy, rigid seams. Today, knitters typically use what we refer to as steeks in stranded-knit garments. Steeks are extra stitches that are added to garments knitted in the round. These stitches can be cut later to create armholes and necklines. The raw edges of the cut steek are folded inside the garment to form a facing. However, a number of other construction methods were used in the Shetland Isles. For the Unst jumper, I chose to separate the front and back at the armholes and work the pieces flat on right and wrong sides. I find this method tedious but well worth the extra time. The armhole seams are supple and strong, and create neat lines when working with lightweight knitted fabric.

The diversity of fleeces available from Shetland sheep in Shetland and elsewhere makes for endless opportunities to experiment with color and texture in handspun yarns and fabrics. As you spin, you can dream about the sheep, grazing on heather amongst the peat cuts in an ancient, rocky landscape.

Keep Reading

Abrams, Lynn. *Myth and Materiality in a Woman's World: Shetland 1800–2000.* Manchester: Manchester University Press, 2005.

Shetland Wool Brokers

A great way to explore worsted yarns in traditional Fair Isle or Shetland knitting is with Shetland combed tops available from Jamieson & Smith. Spinning these beautiful tops into a fingering-weight two-ply yarn will allow you to use many of the Fair Isle patterns available. Jamieson & Smith, known to Shetlanders as the Wool Brokers, continues to support Shetland sheep producers by developing markets for the unique fleeces and making these special yarns and fibers available beyond Shetland's coastlines.

CHAPTER TWO:

From Raw Fleece to Rolag

2

Throughout history, cultures producing and using wool have existed in many different landscapes and have created textiles for many different reasons. The availability of tools, access to resources such as water, and the types of sheep that thrive locally are all factors that have shaped textile cultures of the past and present, leading to huge differences in how wool can be handled. Spinners can be left feeling overwhelmed when they read conflicting accounts as to the "right" way to wash or prepare a fleece. While this diversity of ideas might seem confusing, it can also give handspinners more opportunities to explore the many techniques for preparation, spinning style, and end use. Traditional and common knowledge should serve as strong guides but should not limit a handspinner's explorations.

Skirting and Sorting Fleeces

Many spinners find that fleece acquisition can quickly outpace the time we have to wash and spin the lovely fibers we add to our stashes. At the very least, new fleeces should be unrolled, inspected carefully, and skirted (if they are not already) before storage. Skirting refers to the process of removing less desirable wool and debris from a fleece, which are typically around the margins of a fleece. To skirt is to remove these margins: neck, leg, and belly wool tend to have much shorter staples and are prone to catching bedding, dirt, and hay. Wool around the sheep's tail is removed if there are dung tags (manure caught in the locks, also called "dags" in many regions) or sweat locks (locks filled with suint and lanolin).

If you're new to working with raw fleeces, it can be a bit alarming to unroll a fleece and try to, quite literally, make heads or tails of it. If the fleece was rolled in classic fashion, the fleece will typically have the shorn edge of the locks facing out with the neck end of the fleece on the outside of the roll. Some types of fleeces, such as Shetland, can also be rolled with the tips of the locks facing out. As the fleece is unrolled, it will end with the tail area of the fleece, and the sides of the fleece can be folded outward. Some types of fleeces, such as luster longwools, are more difficult or impossible to keep in a tidy fleece shape and fall into a beautiful, yet jumbled, pile of locks. This is the nature of some lock formations and not a reflection on the shearer or shepherd's wool handling.

Once unrolled, look for the finer, often fuzzier neck fibers and the often coarser, dirtier fibers from the britch and tail areas. The center back will often be more weathered and chaffy than the wool that grew on the sides of the sheep. If the fleece wasn't rolled, try to lay the fleece flat and then search for the finest area that might have some extra VM (neck), and this should be opposite the coarsest area (tail and back legs).

Purchasing fleeces that have already been skirted is ideal because you will not be paying for unusable wool. However, there are plenty of cases where fleeces will not be skirted or might not be skirted as well as you might like. And this poses the question—how much skirting is enough? On some fleeces, there will be a clear line between usable and unusable wool. More often, there is a transition area between, for instance, fairly dirty, short belly wool and beautiful fleece that grew on the sheep's sides. How much should be removed? Some thrifty spinners will keep more of the fleece, avoiding waste, while others spinners will skirt more and not allow marginal wool to diminish the rest of the fleece's quality. This is a personal

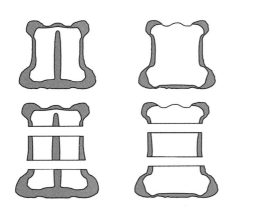

Skirting and sorting strategies, where the gray areas indicate wool to be removed. You might choose to do a lot of skirting (top left) or only a little (top right). Fleece character can vary throughout a fleece. You might choose to sort these areas and process them separately (bottom left and right).

ROLLING A FLEECE

Unrolled fleece with the tail of the fleece at left and the head at right.

To roll a fleece, start with the fleece lying cut side down for most breeds. Identify the neck and tail areas with the center back like a line between them. Fold the sides of the fleece into the center so they overlap on the center back.

Begin rolling the fleece from the tail (where the wool is usually coarser) toward the neck.

Once rolled, twist a piece of the neck wool into a point that can be tucked into the fleece to secure the roll.

THE PRACTICAL SPINNER'S GUIDE: **WOOL**

question and with experience becomes clearer. Sorting a fleece can aid the process. When working with larger fleeces or multiple fleeces similar in breed and character, each fleece can be divided and sorted by quality—crimp character, fineness, color, and staple length. As discussed in the previous chapter, sheep fleeces are not homogenous from one end to the other. In some breeds, consistency in fleece character from nose to tail is very important, while for others inconsistency is more acceptable. Sorting a fleece keeps parts of the fleece with similar character and staple length together, creating more consistent lots of fiber. Shorter, finer fibers from the neck and shoulder are perfect for knitted lace, while the fleece from the sides might make a beautiful sweater. If the hind end of the fleece is coarse, it can be spun and woven into hard-wearing rugs. This approach works well if you have large fleeces or several similar fleeces to combine. You might choose to leave smaller fleeces unsorted so you have enough fiber for a given project.

During skirting and sorting is the time to look the fleece over carefully and check for common fleece problems, moisture, insects, etc.

A tidy fleece at Jamieson & Smith's wool sorting room in Lerwick, Shetland.

Next Steps

After the fleece is skirted, it's time to make some decisions. Are you going to store your fleece or use it now? Either way, there are as many opinions about how to store, wash, and process fleeces as there are handspinners. Here are some common approaches.

Storing Unwashed Fleece

Fleeces that will not be washed soon are best stored with limited exposure to air. As the lipids (oils, waxes, and such) oxidize, they become harder to remove from the wool fibers and can leave a gummy residue. Many experienced spinners find that unbleached cotton or canvas bags work well, while others use airtight containers such as plastic buckets with lids. Either way, a fleece that is firmly packed, rather than loose and exposed to more air, will keep better over time. (We'll discuss this in more detail in Chapter 5.)

Spinning Unwashed Fiber

Fleeces can be prepared for spinning without being washed, which is often referred to as spinning in the grease. Fleece can also be soaked to remove much of the dirt and water-soluble suint without removing the hydrophobic grease and waxes (which is done by scouring). The final yarns are typically fully or partly scoured, particularly if they are to be dyed. There are pros and cons to spinning in the grease—read on.

Custom Washing and Processing

Many spinners I meet love to shop for fleeces but don't love washing or preparing them for spinning. Custom carding mills are a great option for strong, healthy fleeces with medium staples. Many mills require a staple length between 2½ and 5 inches (6.5–12.5 cm), with something like 3½ inches (9 cm) being optimal. Fleeces with breaks or fragile tips

---

Spinning in the Grease

Spinning in the grease is less common today in most handspinning communities. In the past, spinning before washing was particularly important in places where fuel and/or water resources were limited. Today, most handspinners have a plethora of ready-to-spin industrially processed fibers available. If we are starting from fleece, we can take advantage of small custom mills that will scour our wool for us, and if washing ourselves, we have the benefit of improved soaps and detergents. However, there are fiber artists who continue to spin yarns for spectacular textiles using unscoured wool. These spinners might take a nice clean fleece and go straight to carding or even add additional oil to the wool, particularly for low-grease fleeces. Others might give the wool a soak in cold to warm water to remove some dirt and dust as well as the water-soluble suint, leaving the grease and waxes behind. The final yarns are often scoured after they are spun.

can be torn by carding machines. The resulting carded roving will be filled with noils and short broken fibers, making it difficult to spin. Some mills also have combing machines that can remove many of the noils, short fibers, and debris, yielding a smaller amount of higher-quality fiber in the end. (We'll discuss this in more detail in Chapter 3.)

Handwashing and Processing

Washing and processing your own fibers takes time and work, but for many spinners, it can be as pleasurable an occupation as the spinning itself. Other spinners may prefer spinning over washing and combing but find that the time and energy invested in careful preparation is well worth the satisfaction of spinning silky, spotless combed tops.

Washing Wool

Why wash? There are many very good reasons for washing wool prior to preparation and spinning. Pests such as wool moths are more attracted to raw fibers than washed fibers. Note that this doesn't mean that moths will not happily take up residence in clean fleeces, but the scent of raw wool is as enticing to moths as it is to many a handspinner. Much smaller beasts are of concern as well. There are several zoonotic diseases that handspinners should keep in mind. Zoonotic means that these are diseases that animals, sheep in this case, can pass to humans. Just use common sense and basic sanitation, like washing your hands after sorting fleece. Contagious ecthyma (commonly called soremouth in sheep), dermatophytosis (ringworm, which is actually a fungus), and Caseous lymphadenitis (often simply called CL by shepherds) can be contracted through small cuts on your hands or arms.

While these diseases are very, very rarely contracted through fleece handling, take care to cover any exposed cuts before unrolling your fleece on the skirting table. Anthrax can also be harbored in shorn fleeces but is exceedingly rare.

And last, but not least, a washed fleece that has had as much nonwool material removed as possible (suint, wax, dirt, manure, etc.) is typically easier to prepare and spin into a consistent yarn. The waxes naturally present in wool begin to oxidize once shorn, becoming less fluid and much stickier with time and making spinning and washing more difficult. The process of fully removing dirt, water-soluble substances (suint), and non-water-soluble substances (wool wax) from fleece is called scouring. When a fleece is scoured, it will generally lose between 30 and 50 percent of its weight. The percentage of wool that remains is referred to as the yield. Yields vary not only from breed to breed but can also fluctuate within a flock. Scouring prior to spinning means that these major changes in weight and character happen before you create the yarn you want.

Scouring has been accomplished in a number of ways through history, but today we tend to stick with hot water and a soap or detergent. The process itself isn't difficult but does need to be tailored a bit for where you live and what you are washing. Let's start by looking at the main factors involved in typical scouring.

Water

The chemistry of the water used for scouring impacts how well different types of soaps and detergents work. This is a fascinating and complex subject, and if you are interested in learning more, *Wool: Science and Technology* edited by Simpson and Cranshaw is a great place to start. For handspinners processing wool at home, just having a general idea about your water's chemistry can be helpful. A quick online search for water hardness maps for your region should point you in the right direction. Whether you are using rainwater, surface water, or well water to wash fleeces, each will have a measure of hardness. There are different types of hardness, but to keep it simple, hardness refers to the amount of calcium and magnesium present in the water, which can be accompanied by metals such as iron. These minerals reduce the effectiveness of soap and some detergents, so harder water makes washing more difficult. Water picks up minerals as it filters down through the soil, so the amount and type of minerals present depend on the soils in your area and whether your water came from a surface or groundwater source. Many people who have hard water install water softeners in their homes. Softeners remove most of the calcium and magnesium from the water, helping household detergents work more effectively and keeping mineral scale from building up on showerheads, tea kettles, and the like. If you are part of a municipal water system, information about water treatment and quality is often available online.

Soap and Detergents

When scouring fleece, soaps and detergents are used to separate the wool wax from the wool fibers. When wool is placed in hot water with detergent, the lipids (wax, grease, oil) are emulsified. This means that the wool wax is pulled off of the fibers and is suspended in the water. The wool can then be removed, free of the wax and dirt, which remain in the water. If you have soft water or hard water that has been softened effectively, this process is fairly straightforward. If you have hard water or very hard water, finding the

Check the Label

When using washing products not designed for wool scouring, such as dish and laundry detergents, most spinners avoid products listing helpful enzymes, optical brighteners, or bleach.

right detergent is key. Why? Hard water will react with natural soaps, creating the dreaded soap scum, a residue you definitely don't want in your fleece. Synthetic detergents were developed to improve washing in a wider variety of water types. Common washing agents such as those used for laundry or dishes typically contain anionic or nonionic detergents—and often some of each. Nonionic detergents are the most effective if you have very hard water, but anionic detergents will still be much more effective than soap in hard water.

How much soap or detergent do you need? This will depend greatly on your water, soap or detergent type, and fleece. If you are using a product designed for scouring wool, the label will give guidance on how much product to use. If you are using a dish detergent (Dawn is a favorite among handspinners) ¼ cup (60 ml) is a good place to start for a pound or two of moderately greasy fleece per wash. Adjust as needed.

Temperature

Water temperature is very important when washing wool. Research shows that wool wax begins to melt at 110°F (43°C); however, a minimum effective scouring temperature is usually between 120°F and 140°F (49 and 60°C). Many woolen mills scour fleeces closer to the 160°F (71°C) range. One of the most common problems spinners have with scouring is when the fleece is left to soak so long that the temperature drops and the wax begins to redeposit onto the fibers. Remember that as soon as the water is drawn, it is cooling. Fibers don't need to sit in the wash for more than 15 minutes or so. If scouring in buckets or pots where heat loss is rapid, cover with a lid during scouring to keep the temperature up.

Bringing It All Together

Successful scouring is about balancing temperature and detergent for your water and fleece. Water temperature and washing agents are easy to adjust when fine-tuning your scouring regimen. Fine, greasy fleeces often require more detergent and higher water temp than luster longwools or Down-type fleeces. Where I live in Indiana, we have very hard water that also has a high iron content. I've found that using more than one type of detergent can help me get fleeces cleaner. When washing luster longwool fleeces from my flock of Border Leicesters, I do one scour using an eco-friendly laundry detergent and a second scour with either dish soap or a wool wash. I find that using more than one detergent gives me better results than simply using higher temperatures, which can leave these fleeces feeling a bit brittle and harsh.

I also adjust the ratio of water to raw wool based on what type of wool I am washing. I use a higher ratio of water to wool when scouring fine, greasy fleeces. I do most of my washing in a double utility sink. To wash two pounds (900 g) of moderately soiled or greasy fleece, I fill a tub about half full—between 6 and 10 gallons (20–40 L) of water. Some spinners use dramatically more washing liquor, while others use much less. Experiment and see

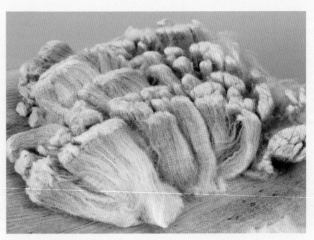

Fleece ready for washing.

what you like best. When learning, it's good to start off with less wool per scouring bath until you get comfortable with the process.

Preparing and Managing Fiber for Washing

Fleeces can be washed as a loose mass or kept in careful alignment depending on how the fiber will be prepared for spinning. If a fleece is to be combed and spun into a smooth, sleek yarn, the fiber should be handled in a way that keeps the locks intact. If the fleece is to be teased and carded for woolen spinning, lock formation isn't as important.

Washing Locks Individually

This works especially well for very fine wools that will be spun into very fine worsted yarns. I learned to wash locks in this way from Margaret Stove, a fine-lace spinner and knitter from New Zealand. Margaret is much beloved in the handspinning community and shares her washing method in her DVD *Spinning for Lace*.

Start with two small tubs of water. The first tub is used for washing and should be about 176°F (80°C). The second tub is for rinsing and doesn't need to be quite as hot. Margaret stresses that if the wash water is not hot enough or begins to cool, "the lock will want to float on the surface and the grease in the wool will not melt and combine with the soap to wash away." Hold each lock firmly by the cut end, dip it in hot water, and then scrub it vigorously on a bar of soap. Swish the soapy tip in rinse water. Next, hold the lock by the tip and repeat the process for the cut end. Press the wet lock with a towel to remove excess water and allow to dry.

Works well for: Very fine fleeces. I find that when working with an uncoated fine-wool fleece that has some VM near the tips, the swishing action of the lock in water when holding the cut end can actually allow quite a bit of matter to move out of the lock.

Drawbacks? The primary disadvantage to washing lock by lock is that it is a slow way to wash a fleece. However, when spinning super-fine yarns, each lock can yield yards and yards of beautiful yarn.

WASHING LOCKS INDIVIDUALLY

Separating locks from fleece.

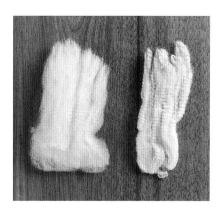

Lock washed using Margaret Stove's method (left) and unwashed lock (right).

Washing Small Groups of Locks

This has become a common washing method used by handspinners, especially for fine fleeces. Locks are organized and wrapped in some type of netting. This keeps the locks organized and ready for worsted spinning. One section of the fleece can be placed into a zippered mesh bag (such as a lingerie bag), or locks can be separated from the fleece and laid on a piece of tulle fabric in neat rows. The tulle can then be rolled and pinned into a tidy package often referred to as a tulle sausage.

Works well for: Crimpy wools that will easily move out of lock formation during washing. If you plan to comb or flick the locks for worsted spinning, this method keeps everything orderly and allows you to wash many locks at one time.

Drawbacks? This method, too, is considered labor-intensive by some spinners.

Washing Unorganized Small Batches

This is a great compromise for efficiency and dealing with fleece disruption. Zippered mesh bags come in a variety of sizes, but the larger versions will comfortably hold about a half pound of wool. The fiber can be a bit condensed but shouldn't feel packed. These zippered bags also allow you to move the wool in and out of the bath without disrupting many of the locks.

Works well for: Just about anything that doesn't require perfect lock structure. Typically, the majority of the locks will be in nearly perfect lock formation so they can be easily combed, and the unkempt locks can be used for carding.

WASHING SMALL GROUPS OF LOCKS

Method 1: Place a fleece section into a mesh bag.

Method 2: Lay the locks in neat rows on a sheet of tulle (top), then roll the tulle and secure (bottom).

WASHING UNORGANIZED SMALL BATCHES

Fill the bag about half full of wool to wash.

Drawbacks? If the fiber is too tightly squished into the bag, it can be more difficult to get the center of the wool clean. Also, the restrained movement reduces the amount of VM that can be removed during washing.

Washing Loose Fleece

When washing fleece that is not restrained in bags, it can be helpful to have a way to remove the fleece from the water without agitating or handling the fiber any more than necessary. Some spinners use a screen or tray that is placed in the basin below the fibers. The tray can then be brought to the surface to lift the fiber out of the water and allow it to drain for a few minutes before being placed in the next wash or rinse.

Works well for: Washing larger amounts of fleece. Also, additional VM can sometimes be removed when the fleece has more room to move around.

Drawbacks? Locks can become disarranged, which can lead to tangling and make some types of fiber preparation, such as flicked locks, more challenging.

Sample Washing Procedure

Let's go through a sample washing procedure for a nice, clean Jacob fleece. This fleece is at the fine end of the breed, has fairly consistent character with a 4-inch (10 cm) staple length throughout the fleece, and came from a lovely ewe named Constance. I would like to use Constance's fleece for a laceweight yarn that is worsted-spun from flicked locks. I will use two mesh bags, each containing about ½ pound of wool, to wash about a pound at one time. These instructions will be geared toward washing in buckets or a sink. Wool can be set aside between scours to allow the excess water to drain, but I prefer using a top-loading washing machine to spin out the extra water. If you don't have a washing machine handy, there are great laundry tools available that are basically laundry-scale salad spinners—they work like mini centrifuges.

Step 1: I am a strong advocate for soaking fleeces in cold water for a few hours prior to scouring. This cold soak in just water (no detergent) removes suint, the water-soluble components of a raw fleece. Quite a lot of the dust and dirt will also be removed in this wash. The resulting tea-colored water is high in potassium and can be poured on outdoor plants. When ready to scour, remove the fiber from the cold soak and spin the excess water out or allow to drain.

Step 2: Fill the wash basin with hot water around 140°F (60°C). (This temperature is a good starting place, but it can be adjusted depending on your needs.) Mix in soap or detergent and carefully place the bags in the washing liquor. After about 15 minutes, remove the bags of fiber and spin the excess water out or allow to drain.

Step 3: Repeat Step 2 to scour a second time if necessary.

A fleece will never look worse than when it first comes out of the wash. From left to right: Raw locks, wet washed locks, dry washed locks.

Step 4: Refill the basin with hot water but do not add detergent. Place the bags of fiber into the basin for a few minutes. Remove the bags of fiber and spin the excess water out or allow to drain.

Step 5: Repeat Step 4 at least once. If the fleece feels clean but looks dirty, extra rinses can help dramatically. Spin the excess water out of the fleece or carefully roll in towels.

Step 6: Don't be too alarmed if your beautiful fleece is looking a bit crumpled. Resist the temptation to start picking at VM and fussing over locks—it can cause more harm than good. Wool is weaker when wet, and locks are more likely to become disarranged if handled too much before they dry. Lay the fleece out to dry on a screen or on a towel near a fan. Air movement is more important than air temperature when drying. And remember, one of wool's special characteristics is its ability to hold water and feel dry to the touch. Allow it to fully dry before storing.

Troubleshooting: When It Doesn't All Come Out in the Wash

Wool Is Sticky After Scouring

The first thing to try is rescouring using a higher water temperature. It could also be that the wool remained in the wash too long and began to cool, allowing the wool wax to settle back into the fleece. Another strategy is to try adding more detergent or even trying a different soap or detergent. Also, fleeces from sheep that had irritated skin can have a sticky, gummy feel that is hard to remove without felting or damaging the fleece.

White Globs Appear in Wet Fleece

This white matter might be waxy residue, in which case try rewashing using a higher water temperature. Also try using more detergent or a different soap/detergent altogether. If the white globs are still there, your fleece might have scurf (see Intentional Processing, page 90).

Felted Fiber

If a batch of wool comes out of the last rinse looking a bit felted, lay it out to dry—resist the urge to pick at it until it is completely dry. Sometimes, it isn't nearly as bad as it looks when fully wet. However, if it is still moderately to very felted after it's dry, either learn from the experience and compost the fiber (if the worst thing you ever do is felt 1 pound of wool, it isn't the end of the world) or simply appreciate your new fiber-art object.

Dyeing

Wool can be dyed at any stage of processing—as washed fleece, as unspun fiber, as spun yarn, or as finished textile. Whether you are interested in natural dyeing or synthetic dyeing, there are great resources available. Here are a few to get you started:

Dagmar Klos, *Dyer's Companion* and various DVDs

Deb Menz, *Color in Spinning* and various DVDs

Border Leicester locks that were immersion dyed.

Preparing Fleece for Spinning

To prepare wool for spinning, the fibers need to be loosened from their orientation in the wool lock. This allows the fibers to move smoothly out of the fiber mass and into a consistent yarn. A variety of tools can be used to open the locks and organize the fibers to create different types of preparations. Which preparation you choose depends on the fiber you begin with and the yarn you would like to spin. There are two primary groups of fiber preparations: woolen and worsted. These are like two ends of a continuum, and most of the yarns we spin will fall somewhere in between.

Woolen Preparations

Primary features: Airy and warm, soft, elastic, and fuzzy.

Fiber: Should be shorter than 3½ to 4 inches (9–10 cm) and might contain a variety of fiber types and lengths.

Fiber alignment: The individual fibers should be disorganized or aligned perpendicular to the direction they will be spun.

How does this change my yarns? Woolen preparations can be spun in a variety of ways, but the resulting yarns will always have a bit of a fuzzy halo and generally contain more air, making them lighter weight.

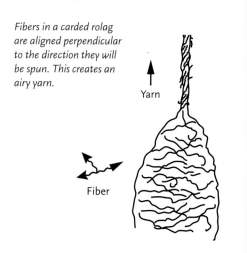

Fibers in a carded rolag are aligned perpendicular to the direction they will be spun. This creates an airy yarn.

Yarn

Fiber

Worsted Preparations

Primary features: Smooth, defined, organized, and dense.

Fiber: Should be longer than about 3 inches (7.5 cm) and all should be the same staple length.

Fiber alignment: The individual fibers should be organized and aligned parallel to the direction they will be spun.

How does this change my yarn? Because the fibers are tidy and pushed together side by side, the yarn will be dense and smooth with fewer fibers sticking out of the yarn.

Whether a fiber preparation is more woolen-like or worsted-like depends not only on the fiber used but also on how the fiber tools are used.

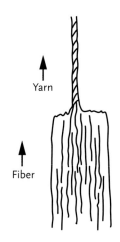

Yarn

Fiber

Fibers in a combed top are aligned in the direction they will be spun. This creates a smooth yarn.

A History of Worsted in Worstead

Understanding the history of the word *worsted* can be helpful in understanding how it is different from woolen preparations and yarns. The term worsted, which can refer to either fiber prep or spinning style, is believed to take its name from a town in Norfolk, England, called Worstead. During the Middle Ages, textile workers from Flanders and the Netherlands were encouraged to settle in Norfolk by King Edward III in hopes that an influx of knowledge and skill would further improve England's cloth manufacture. England was at that time trading large amounts of long, lustrous wool to manufacturers in Europe, where it was combed, spun, and woven into fine cloth. It's thought that with this helpful importation from Flanders, England's worsted cloth industry was improved.

The woolcombers' trade was highly organized and influential until the process began to be mechanized in the mid-1800s—later than some other textile trades. "The decline and extinction of the handcomber" is how John Burnley describes the last chapter of this story in his 1889 tome *The History of Wool and Woolcombing*. Author Peter Teal explains in his book *Hand Woolcombing and Spinning* that when he first became interested in learning about woolcombing in the 1960s, finding tools and information in England was a challenge. Teal has researched archives and collections in his important efforts to learn more about the history of hand woolcombing and has helped to revitalize interest in this important piece of textile history.

Handcarding

Carding is a process of teasing and opening locks, creating a homogenous loosened mass of fibers. It's a great way to blend fibers of various lengths and qualities and organize them somewhat, bringing them into semi-alignment. The degree to which the final preparation is organized will depend on the fibers and techniques used. The carding process can provide us with several types of preparations, but the most common is the *rolag* (pronounced roll-AAG), produced when fibers are rolled off the card and form a loose tube. The idea is that the carded fibers allow us to spin an airier, more consistent yarn than if the fibers were simply teased with our hands. And despite being a relatively simple tool, handcards are wonderfully versatile and can be used to create a variety of fiber preparations. If five spinners were put in a room with a fleece and handcards, I would be very surprised if any two of them had the exact same technique. Take this as encouragement for developing your own technique that works for your tools, your body, and the fibers you use.

In the journey toward satisfying and successful carding, it's helpful to first understand how the carding action works. Handcards are covered in a piece of what is called carding cloth. Many rows of teeth protrude from the carding cloth and each one has a little bend called a knee. When the fiber engages as it is pulled against the knee—this is the carding action.

When fiber is pulled against the knee, the lock is engaged and carding happens.

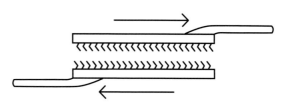

This happens when the cards are facing the opposite direction.

When fiber is pulled away from the knee, it moves easily away from the carding cloth.

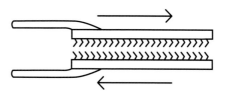

This happens when the cards are facing the same direction.

Types of Handcards

Handcards are available in a range of shapes and sizes, from fairly long rectangles to small, square student or mini-style cards. They can be curved or flat. The wood used varies, changing the weight. Additionally, the carding cloth itself can be quite different from card to card—not only the ppi (points per inch) but also the length of the teeth and thickness of the wire used. Fine-gauge teeth will tend to be a bit more flexible, causing less breakage in the fiber, but stronger wire will card coarser wools faster. My favorite cards for a wide range of wool types are Schacht's 112 ppi curved handcards. For me, the teeth are not too long or too short, too rigid or too supple, and the weight feels good in my hands. Try different pairs of cards and find what fits nicely in your own hands.

Choosing and Preparing Fiber for Carding

For carding, a staple length shorter than 3 or 4 inches will work best. Longer fibers can be carded, but the process becomes difficult. Flicking or combing are more effective for longer fibers. Inspect your fleece for breaks and tender tips. The carding process can tear weakened fibers and will not remove the waste. These torn bits remain in the fiber and can cause noils. Whatever bits of hay, dander, or short fibers are in the wool when it begins the carding process will, for the most part, end up in the finished preparation.

Picking and teasing locks is a great way to prepare fleece for carding. Matted areas, second cuts, and bits of hay can be removed before carding begins, keeping them out of the finished yarn. Since the goal is to remove

Handcards all differ just a bit. From left to right: Schacht curved, Schacht flat, Louet mini cotton.

Teasing locks.

Unteased locks on carding cloth.

Getting Started

Spinners who have spent a lot of time handcarding make the process look effortless. I, like many spinners, didn't love carding at first. It seemed like a slow process and felt a bit awkward, leaving me with stiff shoulders and sore wrists. I spent some time carefully watching people for whom carding seemed as natural as breathing. I watched experienced spinners at demonstrations, searched out videos of spinners in silent films in online museum collections, and pored over old photographs. I eventually developed my own technique that allowed me to create well-carded fibers as efficiently as possible. Successful handcarding is as much about ergonomics as it is about developing the techniques needed to create well-prepped fibers. Take breaks and try alternative ways of sitting and holding the cards if you are experiencing discomfort.

I approach handcarding much like a meditation exercise. As you work, try to keep your body centered and square rather than slouching forward or twisting your core. Make sure you are keeping your posture relaxed with shoulders back. Try to keep wrists straight and engaged but not stressed, allowing your arms to do more of the work. After poring over old photos of spinners with their cards, I learned to hold one card resting on my lap with the handle in my upward-facing palm. When this card is held stationary, resting near my knees in my nondominant hand, my dominant hand can card comfortably without straining my shoulders. Is it possible to create perfectly carded, beautiful fibers if you slouch and hold the cards at eye level? Of course! But you might not be able to card for very long without doing yourself injury. Be good to yourself.

contaminants, make sure you are not teasing locks over your pile of fleece. The extent to which the fiber is picked is truly a testament to our personalities. Some spinners will inspect each lock carefully and tease the fibers open until they are flawless, while others will only do a quick pass through the fiber to open only the more stubborn, matted areas. With clean, easily opened locks, I might even choose to skip teasing. If I am carding wool that is still in lock formation, I often load these locks onto the carding cloth perpendicular to the direction I will be carding. In this case, the handcards are basically doing the picking and teasing step instead of my fingers. After a carding pass, the fibers will change orientation and will be mostly parallel to the carding direction, so the end result is the same as a teased fiber. The difference lies in preparation time. Try several methods and see what will be the best balance of efficiency and quality.

Handcarding Step by Step

While there are many different approaches to carding, the process is basically the same. The three main steps are charging, carding, and removing the finished fibers.

Step 1. Charging the Cards.

Both hands are busy while handcarding, but one hand tends to do more work. Here, I'll call the hand doing most of the work the active hand (which will be your more dominant hand) and the other the passive hand. As a right-handed spinner, my right hand is active, my left is passive. First, we need to put some fiber on the passive card. This is referred to as charging, or dressing, the cards. If the fleece is teased, take a handful of fiber and gently rub it against the center of the carding cloth, moving away from the handle so the fibers engage the teeth. There is no need to press the fibers deeply into the teeth. In fact, if the fibers are pressed too far into the teeth, it is difficult to move them and carding stops. If the locks are distinct, you can also try laying the locks onto the carding cloth perpendicular to the direction of carding, without teasing the locks. Spinners can often be seen orienting the locks in the same direction the cards will be moving, too. Try it several ways and see what you think for yourself. However you decide to charge the card, don't use too much wool at a time. A smaller amount will often work better than struggling with too much.

Step 2. Carding.

Hold the handle of the card in your passive hand with your palm upturned and the card resting on your lap. If this card rests near your knees, your arms will straighten and shoulders will relax. Pick up the other card in your active hand with palm and card facing down. I like to place my thumb and first finger on the back of the card for support. Bring the active card down so the cards are directly above one another (not offset) and the active card is engaged with the fibers on the passive card. The teeth should barely touch. Carding happens between the teeth, not deep in the cloth. Draw the active card backward to begin carding. Repeat this carding motion a few times.

Now you're ready to transfer (remove) the fiber from the active card. Turn the active hand over, so the carding cloth is facing you. Lift the passive card off your lap, and placing the top of the active card against the center of the passive card, move the active card away from your body, lightly engaging the two carding cloths. The fiber should easily peel off the active card and onto the passive card. (If the fiber doesn't easily transfer, see Common Carding Problems, page 74.)

Return the passive hand and card to your lap and resume carding as before. After a few more carding passes, you are ready to transfer

The carding method shown in this photo of Norwegian women in Portland, North Dakota, circa 1892, is a comfortable method for many modern handspinners. Photo by G. T. Hagen, Vesterheim Collection.

the fiber from the passive card. Turn the active card over again and lift the passive card off of your lap. The top of the passive card now meets the center of the active card. Push the passive card forward to transfer the fiber.

How many times should the fiber be passed back and forth between the cards? This really just depends on the fleece quality and how quickly the locks open. Typically two to four passes is sufficient.

Step 3. Removing the Carded Fibers.

When you have decided that the fiber looks consistent and fully carded, transfer fiber to the active card and then all of the fiber to the passive card.

HANDCARDING STEP BY STEP

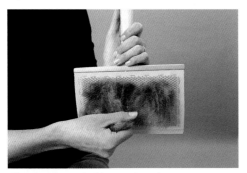

Charging the card with teased wool.

First carding pass.

Transferring fiber from active card.

Transferring fiber from passive card.

ROLLING A ROLAG

Fiber is lying loosely on top of cards.

Lift and tuck to form rolag.

Roll the rolag toward the handle to finish.

Finished rolag on card.

Now there are some decisions to make. The small sheets of carded fibers can be left loose in a basket, ready for spinning, or they can be rolled into a rolag or puni. To roll a very tidy rolag, place one hand on the fiber on the passive card and with the empty card in your active hand, lift the edge of the fibers up. Use your hand to tuck these fibers under as the active card rolls the fiber from the top of the passive card toward the handle into a tidy tube. When the tube reaches the edge of the cloth near the handle, lift the rolag with the passive hand and active card, lay the rolag at

the top of the passive card once more, and roll the active card gently over the fiber toward the handle again. This secures any loose ends and gives the rolag a finishing touch.

To roll a puni (pronounced poo-nee), a term for a tightly rolled tube of fiber, place a dowel or knitting needle at the top of the card. You can also use two dowels with the fiber sandwiched between them. Begin rolling the dowel or pair of dowels down the carding cloth toward the handle, wrapping the fiber fairly tightly. One thing to bear in mind is

ROLLING A PUNI

Rolling a puni, step 1.

Rolling a puni, step 2.

Rolling a puni, step 3.

Rolling fibers sideways on carding cloth.

that the more tightly the fiber is rolled, the more organized the preparation. A more organized preparation reduces the amount of air incorporated into the yarn when spun, creating a denser, less woolen-style yarn.

Additionally, the fibers can be rolled from one side of the card to the other. This is a more worsted-like preparation because the fibers are more or less aligned and oriented in the same direction the yarn will be spun.

From left to right: rolag, puni, carded fibers rolled sideways.

Common Carding Problems

Here are some issues you might encounter when you're carding.

Fiber Doesn't Easily Transfer from One Card to the Other

If the fiber is difficult to transfer, it is usually because it has been pressed too deeply into the carding cloth. Pull the fiber out of the cloth and begin carding again, trying to keep the teeth from pushing the fibers down into the card. Remember, carding is happening between the teeth, not down in the teeth.

Too Much Fiber Near the Handle

This typically happens when the active card engages the passive card too far forward, rather than directly on top.

Too Much Fiber on Top of the Card

There is a little flick of the wrist that can cause this. If cards are not kept parallel and either card rocks away during a carding pass, the fibers can be pulled deeper into the cloth just at the top of the card. Fiber can build up in a ridge in the first few rows of teeth, which will then show up as a thick spot in the rolag.

Fiber Caught or Folded

This can happen in two different ways, but the root cause is the same. The longer the staple of the fiber being carded, the broader the carding motions must be. If the active card does not continue moving away from the passive card far enough that the fibers pulled between them release, the tips of these fibers will be carried forward with the active card during the next carding pass. This folds them forward, creating a thick spot in the rolag. Likewise,

Fibers wrapped around card heel.

Fiber builds up in a ridge.

Fibers being folded during carding.

if the fibers at the top of the active card are folded under when it engages the passive card, a thick spot will form.

Fiber Is Difficult to Control

If carding seems difficult to manage, chances are you have too much fiber on the cards. Locks of wool can be quite dense, and it is easy to unintentionally overload the cards. If this happens, just pull some of the wool off the cards, put it back in the pile to be carded, and continue on your way.

Oy—Static!

Static can be a pesky problem for some spinners depending on where you live. During the winters in Indiana, I keep a spray bottle of clean water in my studio. If I am dealing with static, I just mist the air near my work. If that isn't enough, I lightly mist the fibers.

Take It Easy

Carding should be gentle and nearly silent. You should hear the "shhh" sound of fibers moving through the teeth but not a loud scraping sound as the two cards dig into one another and, above all, you should not hear the fibers ripping and breaking. The teeth of the two cards should barely engage. Remember, once the fiber has been pushed deeply into the teeth, against the cloth, it is hard to reach and carding ceases. This is made much easier when a moderate amount of wool is on the cards. If you are having trouble, try reducing the amount of fiber on the cards.

Flick Carding and Combing Locks

Flicking or combing locks requires very little equipment and is simple to do. These techniques are especially useful if spinning for color effects that begin in the lock such as variegated dyed locks or a natural-color fleece. Spinning lock by lock allows colors and fleece character to be as distinct as possible, so variegations will show in the finished yarn. This can also be a drawback of these techniques if you are striving to spin the most consistent yarn possible. Both flicked and combed locks fall within the worsted preparation sphere because the fibers are aligned. There are many semiworsted techniques, and most experienced spinners agree that a true worsted (or full-worsted) preparation would align the fibers as well as remove any short fibers. The two methods outlined here will differ in how many short fibers are removed, but both will result in a far more organized spinning fiber than a woolen preparation such as a rolag.

The primary difference between flicking locks and combing locks is the direction in which the tool meets the fiber. In flicking locks, the teeth of the flick card move mostly vertically, perpendicular to the staple. When combing locks, the tool moves through the fiber parallel to the staple in a brushing motion. The two methods may produce similar results when using locks that are clean and easily prepared. The difference can be dramatic when working with imperfect fleeces. Combing locks tends to result in more fiber loss but can also remove more vegetable matter, short fibers, and tender tips, and will loosen areas of the lock that are slightly cotted (or felted).

Types of Flickers

Flickers, or flick cards, come in a variety of shapes and sizes. The carding cloth is covered in wire teeth that are slightly bent, just like those on handcards, but flick cards are smaller than handcards. The stiffness of the teeth varies widely by maker, as do the opinions of experienced spinners on which is best. I keep an assortment of flickers so I can choose the one that works best for the type of fiber I am working with at the time.

Flicking a Wool Lock

Use a piece of denim, leather, or cardstock to protect your lap while you flick. I like to hold the lock of wool between my ring finger and middle finger and then pinch the end between my thumb and first finger. The goal is to hold the lock securely enough that none of the fibers are pulled away and tangled.

Bring the flicker down onto the tip of the lock.

With a flick of the wrist (so to speak) move the flicker up and out of the lock.

Avoid dragging the teeth through the fiber horizontally, as this would be combing. Instead, think of bouncing up and out of the lock. Repeat this patting motion once or twice, turn the lock around, and repeat for the other end. If the lock is not open after a few flicks on each end, try smaller locks. If you are still left with neps, too much VM, or tangles, try combing the lock.

Tools for Combing

Different types of tools can be used to comb locks. The classic book *In Sheep's Clothing* refers to this technique as handcombing using a single comb. A dog comb, flicker, or

Tools for flicking and combing locks.

even a fork may be used while holding the lock as if to flick. Alternatively, the tool can be held stationary while the lock is drawn through the comb—this was how I was taught to prepare locks for spinning Shetland lace. Alden Amos covers how to comb a lock using a wool comb or hackle clamped to a table in the *Big Book of Handspinning*, and Maggie Casey uses a handcard in *Start Spinning*. The latter method is the technique I use most often. Using a stationary handcard is similar to working with teasing boards that clamp on a table. I usually sit at a table with a curved handcard on a tea towel.

Combing a Wool Lock with a Flicker

Hold the lock as described for flicking. Instead of bouncing the flicker, draw it through the lock in a brushing motion. Turn the lock around and repeat.

FLICKING A WOOL LOCK

Holding a wool lock for flicking.

Bring the flicker down onto the tip of the lock to engage it.

Move the flicker up and out of the lock to release it.

COMBING A WOOL LOCK WITH A FLICKER

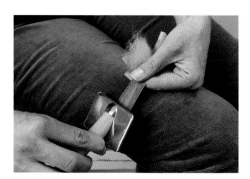

Draw the flicker through the lock in a brushing motion.
Some tangles and VM will be caught in the carding cloth.

Combing a Wool Lock with a Handcard

Hold a handcard on your lap or place it on a flat surface. Hold the lock as before or give the lock a twist and pinch the twist in the center of the lock.

Draw the cut end of the lock through the card once or twice. Turn the lock and repeat. Why the cut end first? Because of the wool cuticle, it will be a bit more resistant to carding. The tip end tends to pull through more easily.

Combing with Woolcombs

Woolcombs are used to loosen fibers from lock formation and bring them into close alignment. Despite combing's importance to textile history, carding has been more commonly used by handspinners in the last hundred years or so. In many places, carding so completely supplanted combing that the knowledge was lost or nearly so. It's meaningful to remember that by the middle of the nineteenth century, worsted machine-spun yarns were available and could be used in combination with homespun in handcrafted textiles. In Norway, Estonia, and many other regions, machine-combed, worsted-spun embroidery yarns in vibrant synthetic colors could be used to embellish woolen-spun cloth made in the home.

One thing to note about woolcombing is that the goal is to produce a fiber preparation, and subsequent yarn and cloth, that is as close to perfection as possible. And in pursuit of perfection, more waste is created by woolcombing than other types of fiber processing. The goal is to remove all of the noils, tangles, short fibers, and imperfections, leaving the remaining wool clean and smooth. This combed top can then be used to spin a smooth, dense yarn. Combing losses of up to 50 percent might raise a spinner's eyebrows but are not unreasonable to many experienced

COMBING A WOOL LOCK WITH A HANDCARD

Twist the lock in the center.

Draw the cut end of the lock through the teeth.

woolcombers. But spinners tend to be thrifty, and what is considered combing waste is sometimes nice enough to use for carding and can always be used for felting or stuffing. Wool is also a natural, renewable resource. It will compost slowly but effectively and can be used by some birds to make colorful nests!

Types of Woolcombs

Today, a wonderful range of combs is available to spinners, from minicombs to massive English combs, entry-level to

Safety tip: Before working with these fiber-preparation tools, make sure your tetanus shot is up to date!

top-of-the-line equipment, and everything in between. Navigating the types of combs and how to best use them starts with understanding the terminology. The long metal tines (also called teeth or nails) vary not only in how closely they are placed but also in thickness and shape. Some companies produce tines that are the same gauge from the base nearly to the tip, ending in a short, sharpened point, while other tines will be tapered from base to tip. Some combs have incredibly sharp tips, while others will be much less so. The shape of the tip can affect the way the wool feels as it is worked, making each style unique. The tines are placed in rows, and a row of tines is referred to as a pitch. Woolcombs with two rows of tines

may be described as two-pitch combs, and woolcombs commonly used today range from one to five pitch. Some of the comb styles available to spinners today are shown below.

Minicombs

Small handheld combs, often called minicombs, are a great way to get started. Being fairly small, they hold a very manageable amount of fiber while you get comfortable with combing. Spinners who do a lot of combing are likely to also have larger woolcombs to process more fiber at one time, but lightweight minicombs are popular for finer fibers, travel and workshops, or when heavier woolcombs might strain tender wrists and hands. Also, some minicombs have fairly dull points. This will impact the way the tines enter some types of fiber but can be good if you are spinning directly off of the comb at the wheel or have children in your workspace. Some minicombs can also be clamped to a table for stationary combing.

Midrange Woolcombs

Many modern combs fit into this category. Larger than minicombs, they can process a respectable amount of fiber at a time. There is quite a bit of variance in the number of tines and how they are arranged from maker to maker, so each type will be appropriate for a unique range of fiber from fairly coarse to very fine. Many spinners who enjoy combing find that having more than one type of comb will allow them to process a full range of fleeces. When matching wool types with combs, a general rule of thumb is the more closely spaced tines work best with fine fleeces, and fewer tines more widely spaced are more appropriate for coarser wools. This is very generalized advice, though. Coarse yet silky fleeces, such as Teeswater, work quite well on fairly fine combs. The best way to learn more is to purchase midrange combs and try them out with as many different types of fleece as you can.

Three types of woolcombs. From left to right: 4-pitch English comb, Valkyrie Extrafine, and Majacraft 2-pitch.

English Combs

These massive, sharp combs are similar to the combs that were used by professional wool-combers in England. Some sources indicate that combs used during the medieval period would have weighed up to 10 pounds (4.5 kg). Just imagine wielding 10 pounds of sharpened spikes in a hot room for hours each day! English woolcombs are now generally thought of as being five pitch and are the largest type of modern comb. One comb is always mounted and may be oriented with the tines horizontal or vertical.

Additional Equipment

Handheld combs can be used without any additional gear, but a few extra pieces of equipment can help make combing easier and more productive. Many combs come with a block, pad, or stand so that one comb can be clamped to a table and kept stationary. This can be used throughout combing or just used when the fiber is removed. I find that placing a piece of nonslip fabric (like you might put

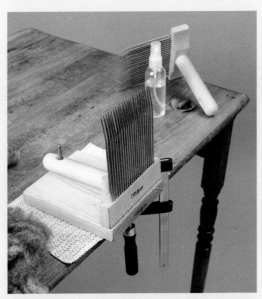

Extra combing equipment: dizzes, comb pad, nonslip fabric, spray bottle, and threader.

under a rug) under the pad can help keep the pad and comb in place. A diz is typically used to remove the fiber into a smooth, consistent combed top. Dizzes can be made of just about anything rigid or semirigid with a hole in the center, but it helps if it is concave. The shape helps funnel fibers to the hole where the fibers are drafted. Some dizzes have different gauge holes so different-size combed tops can be created. It's also nice to have a threader or small crochet hook handy to pull a few fibers into the hole in the diz when drafting begins. Keep a spray bottle with clean water handy to mist your work area if static builds up.

Choosing and Preparing Fiber for Combing

Most of the time, handcombing is used to open and align fibers that are the same staple length and also to separate fibers of different lengths. When combing multicoated breeds such as Icelandic with combs that have fairly closely placed tines like those shown here, the result will be long silky fibers and short, fine fibers. The relative length of these fibers can vary widely from animal to animal, but if there is a difference in fiber length in the lock, the first few combing passes will remove the longest fibers first, leaving the short fibers behind. Combs with fewer, widely spaced tines can be used to tease but not separate these types of wools.

Conditioning Fibers

Quite often, wool is oiled or lubricated a bit before combing. The idea is that oiled wool moves through the combs more easily and forms better tops, while also reducing the static electricity that can develop during combing. Traditionally, olive oil, butter, and the like were used to condition the wool prior to carding or combing. Today, there are many

Lightly misting the fibers with water can help control static.

suggestions from folks who know quite a lot about combing: baby oil, vegetable oil, olive oil, essential oils mixed with water, and more. Additionally, some spinners use a combing milk, a mixture that emulsifies the oil and keeps it blended with water, making it easier to wash out later. (Combed fibers should not be stored for very long if any type of oil is used, as the oils can become sticky or rancid over time.) Some people find that water misted in the area where you are combing is enough to keep static at bay. Water can also be lightly misted directly onto the fibers being combed. If that is not enough, the locks to be combed can be placed in a sealed container and moistened prior to combing to help condition the fibers. Using water instead of oiling the wool means that the combed fibers can be stored for longer periods before spinning.

Heat can be an additional aid in combing. Particularly when the wool is oiled in some way, heated combs can move more easily through the wool as the fibers become more supple. To give it a try, place the tines (but not the wood) of the active comb in hot water prior to use.

Safety First!

It goes without saying, woolcombs can be quite dangerous. And as with any somewhat dangerous activity, the real danger is in forgetting to be careful. I never use my sharp sets of woolcombs when I'm feeling rushed or tired, and I take care to set up my combing workspace before I begin working. Having worked in laboratories while at university, I apply my best lab practices to woolcombing: I don't place anything I need behind the combs so I am not tempted to reach over them; I move anything that might be underfoot that I might stumble over; and I keep fiber and tools on the work surface as much as possible so I don't need to bend down more than necessary (accidentally bumping your head on a set of combs doesn't bear thinking about!).

The only minor accident I've had while combing led me to add one more workspace safety measure when I am clamping a stationary comb or combing pad to a table: I place a piece of nonslip fabric (the kind used under rugs on hardwood floors) under the stationary comb or combing pad. This will help prevent the comb from slipping forward and off the table—a very good thing for fingers and toes! Make sure your tetanus shot is up to date and treat any punctures or scratches when they happen.

THE PRACTICAL SPINNER'S GUIDE: **WOOL**

Combing Step by Step

Step 1. Loading the Combs

Begin by pulling locks from the fleece and finding the tip end. Locks should be loaded (lashed) onto the tines at the cut end of the locks. The last half inch or so of the lock can be pushed into the tines, so that the majority of the lock is now at the front of the combs. If the locks are slightly felted at the cut end from washing or are a bit compacted, I find that my combing waste is reduced if I quickly comb these locks with a flicker or handcard before loading them onto the woolcombs. This opens up the lock a bit, reducing the amount of good wool that might be discarded because of a tangle or neighboring noil. This is also a great time to cut off damaged tips. Some spinners pull the tips off, while others use scissors. Tender tips can break off during processing, causing noils in the fiber and pills in the final textile. So while the locks are nicely arranged on the combs, tip out, just remove the problem with a quick snip. If the tips don't feel dry, look dull, or break when you pull them with your fingers, don't worry about removing them. Lash only a row or two of locks onto the tines of one comb. Whether you are holding both combs or have one mounted onto a surface, think of one comb as stationary and one as active. Your newly loaded comb will be the stationary comb.

Step 2. Combing

During combing, the tines on the two combs should be perpendicular to one another—one is oriented vertically and one is oriented horizontally. (This doesn't always apply to peasant and Russian paddle combs, which are not covered here.) The active comb moves in a circular motion as it engages the fibers. Begin by moving the tines of the active comb into the tips of the fibers loaded on the stationary comb. Once engaged, pull the active comb away from the stationary comb far enough that the newly combed fibers release from the locks. It shouldn't be too hard to pull these combs apart. Try to start at the tips and move closer toward the cut ends with each pass. If the tines enter the locks too deeply, it will be harder to pull, creating more work for you and more stress for the fibers and combs. Continue with this motion until most of the fiber has been transferred to the active comb. Noils, short fibers, and tangles will remain on the stationary comb—pull these off of the tines and place in a waste pile. If static develops, mist the air with water. Now you are ready to transfer the fiber back to the stationary comb. If the tines on the stationary comb are facing up, the active comb will continue moving in a circular motion but will come down onto the stationary comb this time. Once the fiber is mostly returned to the stationary comb, the fiber can be removed. If the comb begins to feel full, the fiber can be removed, and then combing can resume once more. If during this second pass a tangle or stubborn lock ends up on the stationary comb with the finished fiber, you can quickly run the active comb through those fibers to remove it from the finished fiber.

Step 3. Removing the Fiber

Now, you are ready to make a top. Loosen the fibers on the tines of the stationary comb by sliding them up the tines to separate them a bit. The combed fiber can be removed with or without a diz, but a diz can help to compact the fibers and pull them into a more consistent, uniform top.

Without a diz: Pinch the tips of the combed fibers and pull about two-thirds of the staple length straight forward from the comb. If the fibers are reluctant to come forward, try wiggling them back and forth a bit as you pull. Drop the pulled top and pinch once again near

COMBING STEP BY STEP

Flick the cut end of the lock before lashing.

Move the active comb into the tip of the locks.

Pull the comb through the locks until all of the fibers release.

Remove the waste from the stationary comb.

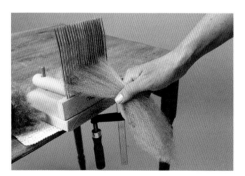

Pulling top without a diz.

Pulling a top with a diz. Pinch the fibers near the diz.

Draw out about a half staple length.

Winding top around your hand.

the tips of the fibers still held by the combs. Pull forward again. Repeat until most of the fiber has been removed. Eventually, shorter or tangled fibers will start to come forward into the top. Stop at that point, and what remains on the stationary comb is waste.

With a diz: Grab a diz and orient it so the concave shape faces away from you; it should behave like a funnel, guiding fibers to the hole in the center. Pull a few of the combed fiber tips through the hole in the diz with a threader or your fingers. Hold the diz stationary so that the fiber tips gently push against it. Pull the fibers straight out through the diz until about half of the staple length emerges. Drop the top, return to the diz, and repeat to draw out another length.

After dizzing, the combed top can be wound into a ball so it stays organized until it is spun. I prefer to spin my combed tops from the cut end of the fiber. Because of the orientation of the cuticle, the fibers slide more

Finished combed top nests.

easily through your hand in this direction. To spin this way, the combed top should be wound into a ball starting from the tip end. Find the tip end (which would be the end first pulled through the diz in this case) and wind the combed top loosely around your hand. When you get to the end of the top (which would be the cut end of the locks), poke it into the center of the nest so you can find it easily when you sit down to spin. I create tidy top nests this way for several reasons. I prefer to spin top from the cut end of the locks, and I often do a lot of combing one day and spin the next. These little bundles can be safely dropped into a basket to await spinning. There are many approaches to combing, and it's important to try several methods to see what works best for you.

Troubleshooting

During combing, the fibers appear to be getting shorter: The fleece you are working with probably has a tender spot and is breaking during combing. A combed preparation is not in this fiber's future. (See Intentional Processing, page 90.)

So much waste! Combing produces more waste than any other fiber-preparation method because it yields a perfect product, or as close to perfect as possible. However, look at your waste fiber carefully. Is it mostly made up of short fibers, second cuts, hay, and noils? Holding the fiber up in front of a window can help you see what is in the mix. If you see quite a bit of nice, strong, full-staple fibers in the waste, there might be something else going on. As in all things, practice makes perfect, and with experience, there tends to be less waste. Good wool can end up with the waste if it gets tangled during combing. Make sure static isn't causing the fibers to spread and become less organized. Also watch that when the fibers are transferred from one comb to the other, the fibers fully release between the combs. If the active comb doesn't move far enough away to disengage the fibers, they will be folded back on the next pass and get tangled. And make sure to start combing the tips of the fibers and work slowly toward the cut end. Inserting the combs into the locks midstaple can cause fibers to build up behind the tines, increasing the percentage of waste.

Fibers don't want to pull through the diz easily: If too much fiber is pulled through the diz orifice at once, it can become jammed. Try holding the diz just a bit farther away from the comb while pulling top. Another reason might be that the fibers have not been separated and loosened a bit on the tines. Slide some of the fibers up the tines a bit to loosen them.

The fibers came off the comb in a big chunk: This might mean that the fiber is too fine for the type of combs used or the fibers were pulled off the top of the tines. Try lashing the fiber onto the tines just a bit farther up the lock, so that more of the cut end of the lock is behind the tines.

Blending Colors and Nonwool Fibers

One of wool's important characteristics is that it blends easily with many other types of fibers. We can mix wool with fibers such as angora or camel down to create an airy yarn with a soft halo, or blend wool with a bit of silk to increase drape and sheen. The natural crimp and cuticle structure of wool aids the blending process and allows us to create blends that are easy to prepare and spin. However, as discussed in Chapter 1, wool fibers can vary dramatically from superfine Merino to the bold, strong locks of a Lincoln fleece. This means that silk blended with Merino, and silk blended with Lincoln can both result in stunning handspun yarns, but they would be strikingly dissimilar. The differences in staple length, crimp, and fineness characteristics of the fibers being blended are very important.

Important Blending Considerations

Here are a few things to keep in mind when blending fibers.

Differences in Staple Length. Dramatic differences in staple length can make blending more difficult. These blends are easier to prepare using cards, creating woolen or semiwoolen preparations. Additionally, when blending fibers with different staple lengths, I find that if other characteristics are more similar, blending is a bit easier. For example, camel down (which might have a 2-inch [5 cm] staple) will usually blend more readily with a fine, crimpy 4-inch (10 cm) wool than with a 4-inch silky longwool.

Two blended yarn samples —one more homogenous (far left) than the other (second from left)—and the fibers used to create them.

Fibers can also be cut to similar staple lengths. This technique is more often used for handcombing because the combing action will tend to separate fibers of different lengths—the opposite of what we want here. Let's say you are planning to blend a bit of silk with a fine Corriedale fleece, and you really want a smooth combed top for spinning crisp yarn for knitted lace. Woolcombs would be a great way to prepare this blend for the intended project. The Corriedale has a 3½-inch (9 cm) staple, but the silk top you choose is about 5 inches (12.5 cm). Cutting the silk to match the length of the wool will allow the two to blend more readily. The cut silk "waste" can be kept for a carding project. This being said, I tend not to cut fibers unless I have a very good reason to do so.

Differences in Fineness. While it might seem logical to try to soften a fleece by blending it with a fine fiber, it doesn't always work that way. Scientists call the effect different fibers and blends have on human skin the "prickle factor." If even 5 percent of the fibers in a woolen garment are coarse (which is, in this case, defined as anything over 30 microns), it can intensely irritate delicate skin. We all have different tolerances for prickles. If you're

Woolen Wanderlust

Today, spinners are spoiled with the many types of wools and other beautiful fibers readily available. With so many combinations of fibers, preparation tools, and blending strategies, there are endless opportunities to discover your own techniques and tricks. Time spent experimenting and sampling is never time lost.

To create a homogenous blend, hold all the colors together as you load them onto the carding cloth.

To create a variegated blend, such as a striped rolag, load the fibers onto the cloth in stripes. Card until the fiber is blended to the desired extent.

planning to make a textile that will be worn next to your skin, spin a small sample and tuck it into your collar for an hour. If you forget it's there, you're good to go.

Degree of Blending. One of the benefits of handblended fibers is that you can choose when to stop blending. Blending less will give a more variegated look to the spun yarn, or you can choose to blend the fibers or colors until fully mixed, yielding a more homogenous effect in the finished yarn.

Blending with Handcards

If all fibers you will combine are shorter than about 4 inches (10 cm), carding is a great way to create a blended woolen or semiwoolen preparation. Carding is also a great way to blend for different color effects. The following strategies build upon the basic carding method outlined earlier in this chapter.

To create a more homogenous blend: When blending several colors of wool into one new shade that is more or less homogenous, I like to quickly card each color separately before combining the colors together. Because the fibers of each color have been opened into a uniform density, the relative amounts of color are easier to control. To create the final blend, hold all the colors together as they are loaded

onto the carding cloth. Card until the colors are fully mixed.

To create a more variegated blend: When you don't want blended fibers to be totally homogenous, begin by carding each color separately as before. When the carded colors are ready to be blended, load the fibers onto the cloth in stripes. With each carding pass, the colors will become more homogenous. When the fiber is blended to the extent desired, stop carding and

A homogenous blend (left) and variegated blend (right) with the individual carded fibers used to create them.

A less homogenous blend that was combed a few times (left) and a more homogenous blend that ws combed more times to blend the fibers (right). Yarns spun from these blends would be quite different.

roll the fiber into a rolag. To maintain consistency, it can help to make note of how many carding passes you do for each rolag. How the fiber is loaded on the handcards (stripes in this last example) can dramatically change how the fibers and colors will appear in the blended fiber and finished yarn.

Blending with Handcombs

If the fibers you are blending are all the same staple length, and that staple length is more than about 3 inches (7.5 cm), handcombing is a good choice for blending your fibers into a perfect combed top for worsted spinning.

To create a more homogenous blend, lash the fibers in alternating layers onto the stationary comb. Begin combing, and when the fibers are sufficiently blended, pull the fibers into a combed top with or without a diz as described above.

To create a more variegated blend, begin by combing each color separately and pulling the fibers off into solid-color combed tops. To blend, lash these fibers again onto the active comb with colors side by side or in layers, depending on the color effect you're going for. Transfer the fibers on the active comb onto the stationary comb and then through

a diz to finish the top. Each time the fiber is transferred, it will become more blended and cohesive.

Additional Blending Tools

Picker. Typically used to open locks of fleece, pickers come in many shapes and sizes. Small, hand-operated pickers for home use are on the market, while mills use large pickers that work at an alarming rpm (rotations per minute). Whatever the size or design, pickers use long tines that disarrange the wool locks, teasing them open. This is often a process that precedes carding, but it is also used to do a rough blending of colors or fibers. The resulting textured cloud (not fully processed) could be spun as is for textured yarns, or carded or combed further depending on the fibers used. Bear in mind that tender, matted, or slightly felted fibers can be damaged by pickers. Many manufacturers suggest that pickers will help remove some VM, but the result will vary depending on design and fleece type.

Drumcarder. Drumcarding is a burgeoning topic. This useful tool has much in common with handcards, functioning on the same basic principle of passing fiber from one carding cloth to another in order to open fibers and distribute them evenly. The fiber preparation that results from drumcarding, a batt, can be spun in several ways and even prepared further to create a more woolen or more worsted-like yarn. (More on this in Chapter 3.) So much can be said on the subject of drumcarders and putting them to best use, I'll point you toward Deb Menz's wonderful book *Color in Spinning* and her DVD *Color Works for Spinners*. It is also important to remember that, like hand-carding, pretty much everything that goes into the drumcarder comes back out again—it will not typically remove a significant amount of VM, noils, or short fibers. If you are looking for a smooth, consistent batt, start with healthy, clean, well-teased fibers. If you are looking for texture and consistent inconsistencies, a drumcarder can do that, too!

Blending board. This interesting tool allows for blending on a carding cloth, much like handcards or a drumcarder, but on a wide, open canvas. There are slight variations between brands of blending boards, but they are all essentially a large piece of carding cloth on a flat surface. Fibers are placed on the cloth and then pushed into place, often with a paintbrush or similar tool. How the fibers are arranged and layered determines the way the colors and textures interact in the spun yarn. After the fiber has been arranged and pushed into the carding cloth, it can be pulled up out of the cloth and treated as a small batt or rolled around a dowel to create a large puni.

Hackle. Increasingly used as a color- and fiber-blending tool, a hackle is typically one or two long rows of tines set into a wooden base, which can be clamped to a table edge when in use. The thickness and length of the tines varies by style and maker, as does the distance between tines, all of which impact the amount and types of fibers the hackle can accommodate. As with handcombs, the closer the tines are together, the finer the fibers they can effectively manage. Adding a pitch, or extra row of tines, also increases the hackle's ability to process finer fibers. Prepared fibers of different colors can be lashed onto the tines and then dizzed. This allows the fibers to be pulled into one top without being combed further, so the fibers and colors remain as distinct as possible. These versatile tools can be used in many different ways to create a wide range of color and texture effects.

BLENDING WITH A HACKLE

Lashing the fibers onto the tines.

Pulling a top with a diz.

Intentional Processing

Flawless fleeces are not a requirement for making beautiful yarns. With time and experience, a spinner can learn which problems are easily remedied and which imperfections are not worth the bother. How much extra work you are willing to invest in a fleece is a personal question. To a spinner in a small urban apartment, the very idea of dealing with 10 pounds of beautiful but chaffy Rambouillet might seem implausible. Yet another spinner with outside workspace and a penchant for thrift might take on this same fleece with pleasure. And then there are the fleeces that appear in our stashes before we know that there is a flaw. We don't always have the luxury of carefully inspecting a fleece in its entirety before committing. Most spinners who work with fleece have encountered this situation at some point, so it's good to know which common problems can be corrected or improved—and whether or not you think it's worth the bother. (For information about these problems, see Chapter 1.)

Felting or Cotting

Light cotting (when the wool begins to felt before it's sheared) will cause the locks to stick together a bit. If the cotting is not very advanced, wash the fleece first and then try hand-teasing these sections to carefully loosen the fibers. The goal is to break as few fibers as possible. If the locks are badly cotted and matted, the fibers will crackle and snap no matter how gently they are handled. These locks can be combed individually (see flicking and combing locks above), removing the shorter, broken fibers and tangles, and then either processed into rolags using handcards or made into top using handcombs.

Felting can easily occur during washing and dyeing, too. Even when fleece is carefully handled while wet, the cut ends of the locks can stick together a bit. If the fleece was accidentally agitated or suddenly exposed to cold water after coming out of hot wash water, the fleece can quickly become unusable. If the cut ends are just stuck together a bit, tease them open with your fingers or use a flicker to loosen tangles.

VM (Vegetable Matter)

For longwool fleeces, quite a lot of chaff will simply fall out during carding or combing. Handcombing in particular is great for chaffy longwool fleeces over 3½ inches (9 cm). For other types of fleeces, a bit of extra fiber preparation can help. First, try carefully shaking the fleece. This can be done before or after washing. I suggest doing this outside—the better it works, the bigger the mess. If you're planning to prepare the fleece in a way that requires the locks to be intact, such as flicking or handcombing, handle the fleece gently. Additionally, before handcarding or handcombing, drag each lock through a carding cloth. You can use handcards or a flicker. VM will usually be concentrated near the tip end. If this is the case, hold the lock firmly by the cut end and draw it through the carding cloth. Much of the debris will stay in the cloth. Repeat this several times if necessary. This is a great way to remove tender tips, lightly cotted areas, and VM while teasing the lock in preparation for handcombs or handcards.

Short Fibers

Multicoated sheep often have very short fibers present at the cut end of the fleece that are the shorn tips of a new growth of undercoat. These fibers are often very soft and silky, and when separated from the fleece are a wonderful luxury to spin into an airy woolen yarn.

However, they can cause noils and make spinning a consistent yarn more challenging. Before carding, hold the lock firmly by the tip end and comb the lock with a flicker or by pulling it through a carding cloth (see Flick Carding and Combing Locks on page 75). The short fibers can be saved for later use.

Dermatitis (Scurf, Scale, Skin Flake, Gunk)

Dermatitis affects sheep for a variety of reasons, and the impact on the fleece can range from a few tiny, dry flakes that fall out when the lock is teased to a substance that can be a bit gummy and difficult to remove. The latter is usually referred to by handspinners as scurf, but terminology varies. Scurf is considered a flaw in the fleece, and the effort a spinner makes to avoid a flawed fleece is a personal decision.

When wet, the gunk is much more noticeable, so spinners often discover a problem during washing. The first step is to rewash the fiber using hotter water. Do a hot, soapy wash and rinse, leaving the fiber in each bath for only about 15 minutes. If the gunk is wool wax, the hotter temperature should take care of the stubborn residue. If the gunk remains, you likely have a problem fleece. If you're interested in forging ahead, there are a few tricks you can try. If the debris is dry and flaky, try combing a lock with a flicker or drawing it through the teeth of a handcard. If the debris comes out, prepare each lock in this way before either carding or combing, or simply spin the combed lock. If the scurf doesn't come out with this level of effort and has a sticky, gummy feel, determine where in the lock the scurf resides. Most of the time it will be concentrated at the cut end of the lock. If your lock has a generous staple length, you might consider cutting the lock. I once inherited a beautiful black BFL fleece that had a large amount of scurf in the cut end. The locks were about 5 inches (12.5 cm) long, and the scurf was concentrated in the last half inch (1.3 cm). Because this was a beautiful, strong fleece that I really wanted to use, I sorted out the best 5 or so ounces of fleece. For each lock, I cut the half inch of staple containing scurf from the cut end before loading the now 4½-inch (11.5 cm) locks onto handcombs. The resulting combed top was stunning and free of debris.

Damaged Tips

The tips on uncoated fleeces can become quite brittle, depending on where the sheep lived and how the flock was managed. Damaged tips will often pull off quite quickly when combed with a flicker or handcard. If using woolcombs, lash the fibers onto the combs for use and simply snip the dry, brittle tips off with scissors.

Staining

A fleece with yellowed or stained areas that is otherwise healthy can be a wonderful opportunity to dye variegated locks. Locks with yellowed tips dyed blue will yield locks that transition from blue to green. Likewise, the locks can be spun undyed, and the finished yarns can be tossed in the dyepot—an easy way to achieve a beautiful result!

Stained locks before (left) and after (right) dyeing. Stained tips can add interest to variegated, dyed locks.

Working with wool:

Golden Hour Bag

Where does inspiration come from? This project was born when I opened a beautiful bag of dyed fleece at my local fiber shop and was suddenly immersed in a vivid memory of Venice. Warm olive bread in hand, I am watching the Golden Hour (the last hour of sunlight) slip by, the Grand Canal filling with light. Needless to say, I purchased this magical bag of Polwarth locks. The handpainted locks also remind me of some of my favorite paintings: John Singer Sargent's Venetian watercolors are full of dappled light, lavender shadows, and golden, glowing walls. I love designing textiles based on places or memories, so I stuck with this Venetian theme through the entire project.

After spinning several sample skeins, I decided that the best way to preserve the watercolor effect of merging and evolving color in my yarn would be to comb each lock (a bit different from flick carding; see Combing a Wool Lock with a Flicker, page 77, for details). Using handcards or woolcombs to prepare multiple locks at a time would have blended the colors more than I wanted for this project. Combing each lock creates a worsted preparation and keeps the fibers close together, leaving the colors as vivid as possible in the final yarn.

Fiber Preparation and Spinning

I divided the dyed fleece into three colorways before spinning—reds, lavenders, and plummy browns. As I combed the locks, I paid attention to the cut and tip ends of the locks and laid them into piles oriented in the same direction.

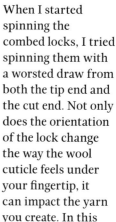

When I started spinning the combed locks, I tried spinning them with a worsted draw from both the tip end and the cut end. Not only does the orientation of the lock change the way the wool cuticle feels under your fingertip, it can impact the yarn you create. In this case, I found that if I spun the locks with the cut end toward the wheel, the fine Polwarth fibers were pushed closer together as I spun the yarn using a short forward worsted draw. By spinning with the cut end first, my fingers slide along the yarn with the grain of the fiber cuticle. A wool cuticle feels the same as human hair. It is smooth moving away from your head but feels "grabby" from tip to root. Also note that this applies to wool that is still in lock form and not to carded preparations or commercial combed top. Because the fibers spun in this way were closer together, the colors in the final yarn were actually more vivid. I always rewind my bobbins onto storage bobbins before plying when I spin locks from the cut end. When rewound, the fibers in the singles were now oriented so the cut end would arrive first at the wheel.

Knitting

I wanted to work the yarns into a stranded knitting pattern, so if these colorful Polwarth skeins were the background, I would need another yarn for the pattern that would contrast strongly. A high-contrast color, like black, wasn't the look I was going for, so I chose to use a texture change to help the pattern "pop." In the end, I chose a golden 50 percent bombyx silk/50 percent Merino combed top to use as the pattern color—very much in keeping with my original Venetian theme. I charted the stitch pattern from the brickwork facade of the Palazzo Ducale in Venice, Italy. In the end, I have a textile that will sweep me back to the sunny days and sparkling canals of my Venetian adventures each time I hold it in my hands.

The Golden Hour Bag was originally published in *Spin·Off* magazine in Spring 2012.

Working with Prepared Fibers

3

As never before, we have clean, ready-to-spin fibers from around the globe at our spinning fingertips. We can find perfectly prepared combed tops processed abroad as easily as we can commission a made-to-order blended batt from an independent fiber artist. Working with prepared fibers can be deliciously indulgent—the fiber's long journey through production, washing, dyeing, and processing is complete, and now it is up to you to dream, scheme, and create. However, not all prepared fibers are a pleasure to spin. Knowing what to look for and what to avoid, as well as what to do with problem fiber, can help smooth the journey.

Purchasing Prepared Fibers— What's Available?

Many great ready-to-spin fibers are available today. The range of prepared fibers available from shepherds, indie fiber artists, and large fiber companies is always growing, much to a spinner's delight!

Where to Find Fibers

Many spinners do not live in an area that has a local fiber shop. The Internet has played a fascinating role in the growth of our textile communities by connecting fiber producers and retailers with consumers. Websites such as etsy.com and localharvest.com are great ways to connect with small-scale fiber producers and fiber artists. However, just remember that purchasing fiber without seeing and handling it in person always has an element of risk involved. One person's "fiber with a little VM" is someone else's "VM with a little fiber." Festivals, conferences, and retreats continue to play important roles in our handspinning communities. Not only do we have the opportunity to gather and exchange ideas at these events, but we often have the opportunity to purchase fibers in person as well. And between gatherings, many spinners spend time on ravelry.com sharing spinning quandaries, new favorite fibers, and project ideas.

Rolags and Punis

Hand-prepared rolags and punis have become popular items in the online shops of independent fiber artists and can be works of art themselves. These specialty fibers can range from very smooth to quite textured blends. Each tube of fiber is typically prepared using handcards or a blending board. When the fibers are removed from the carding cloth, they can either be rolled like a traditional rolag, or wrapped around a wooden dowel to create a puni, compacting the fibers and giving a smoother finish. Both methods are traditionally used to create woolen preparations for woolen-style spinning.

What to look for: Thick or thin spots in the fiber prep can make spinning a consistent yarn more difficult. Even if using a blend incorporating texture, with silk noil for example, look for punis and rolags with a consistent amount of fiber from one end of the preparation to the other. Also note that the more distinct and less blended the fibers are,

Rolags (left) and punis (right).

Carded batts.

the more distinct and separate they will be in your yarn. This is often used as an intentional design element.

Carded Batts

A carded batt is a woolen preparation created using a drumcarder or commercial-scale carding machine. Drumcarders range from small to large and can be operated with a hand crank or powered with an electric motor. As the fibers are fed onto the drum, they wrap in layers, forming a batt. The blended fiber is then typically removed from the drum in one cohesive sheet. Batts can be further prepared for spinning in any number of ways.

What to look for: Batts range from super-smooth, highly organized blends of fibers that are mostly parallel, to riotous, barely unified fibers that contain unexpected components such as pieces of fabric, strips of sequined ribbon, and so much more. Textured batts make great textured yarns, but they will be more challenging to spin into something like a consistent two-ply laceweight yarn. Batts prepared by large carders in woolen mills are more typically used in wet-felting or for quilt batts. However, these large, flat sheets of fiber can be used for spinning. They tend to be made up of short fibers and have a more random fiber orientation, which can make them challenging to use for handspinning.

There's More Than One Way to Spin a Batt

Carded batts are typically sold as rolled sheets of fiber, and the spinner must decide what happens next. Depending on the type of fiber and how it is oriented when you begin to spin, it can behave more like combed top (worsted preparation) or more like handcarded rolags (woolen preparation). Here are a few of the many ways batts can be prepared for spinning:

Drafting a Gradient Batt

Roll the batt into a large rolag with colors aligned. Begin drafting the batt by placing your hands a few inches apart and pulling gently until the fiber has drafted about an inch or so. Move along the batt, lengthening the color repeats a little at a time. I like to draft the entire batt from one end to the other two or three times, slowly drafting the fibers into a gradient roving.

Roll the batt into a large rolag.

Pull the batt gently to draft the fiber. Move along the length of the batt, and repeat the process one or two times.

Stripping the Batt

Position the batt so that the fibers are mostly oriented vertically. Grasp a section of fibers at the top edge and pull down about 2 inches (5 cm). Reposition your hands again closer to the break that is forming and repeat. These strips can be attenuated slightly to straighten raw edges.

Grasp the fibers and pull down 2 inches (5 cm) or so; repeat to form a strip.

Continue creating strips with the rest of the batt.

Stripping and Splitting the Batt

Strip the batt and then split the strips into chunks of fiber. These smaller pieces can be spun at random to create a more homogenous skein. The chunks can also be rolled into rolags. If the fibers are oriented sideways as the twist enters the fiber mass during spinning, the yarn will have an airy, woolen-type character.

Strip the batt.

Break the strips in chunks.

Rovings

Roving is one of the most common types of spinning fibers available to handspinners and is one of the best fibers to use while learning. Roving is created by a carding machine. Most of the fibers will be oriented in the same direction, but they will not be straight and orderly as in combed top. What is the difference? When a fleece enters a carding machine, nearly all of the fiber comes back out at the other end as a finished preparation. This means that any second cuts from shearing or tender fibers that are torn during processing will all be mixed up in the roving. Although they will be arranged mostly parallel, the fibers will have a variety of staple lengths and might include noils, very short fibers, VM, etc. Rovings will fall somewhere between woolen and worsted preparations most of the time depending on the staple length and mill process.

What to look for: Look at roving carefully to see if there are tangles or noils present. Pull out a few fibers and check their length. Fleeces that have a weak spot, or simply do not have the tensile strength for mechanical processing, can be torn during carding. The resulting roving will be quite short and uneven, making spinning more challenging. Look for rovings that are clean of debris (scurf and VM), have a fairly consistent staple length, and are easy to draft.

Pin-Drafted Rovings

Pin-drafted preparations are less commonly used by handspinners than roving or combed top, but they can be a joy to spin. In a mill, this intermediate step is used to condense carded fibers prior to combing. The result is a perfect balance between the bouncy, lively feel of roving and the smooth consistency of a combed top.

What to look for: Pin-drafting aligns and condenses the fibers, but only a small amount

Hold the roving up to the light and look for noils. They will look like small clumps of fibers.

of VM and no short fibers are removed during the process. Look for fairly clean pin-drafted roving that is free of noils and has a fairly uniform staple length.

Combed Tops

Fibers that have been combed mechanically can be quite different from combed top prepared by hand. Some custom spinning mills have combing machines, but most of the combed fibers we see on the market today come from large commercial mills. As the fibers in combed tops are attenuated and pulled into alignment during combing, the natural crimp of the wool fiber is subdued. This effect will vary greatly from fiber to fiber and mill to mill. After the yarn is spun and washed, the crimp will be refreshed and can cause your finished yarn to be different than it appeared during spinning.

What to look for: Combed tops that are a bit (or a lot) felted can be difficult to spin into a smooth yarn and can strain your hands during spinning. Much of the hand-dyed spinning fiber available comes in this form, so keep in mind that during the dyeing process, felting can easily occur.

Clockwise from top left: roving, pin-drafted roving, combed top.

Treated Wool Fibers

The most common chemical treatment applied to wool fibers is dyeing, but wool processed in industrial settings can undergo a variety of additional chemical treatments. Two common processes are shrink-proofing and carbonizing. Wool that is shrink-proofed, which handspinners and knitters generally refer to as superwash, has been altered so that the fiber's cuticle can no longer react to heat and moisture, thus preventing or inhibiting felting. Shrink-proofed wool preparations will range from fiber that feels only slightly slick and silky to fiber that is so processed it hardly feels like wool at all. Some spinners don't mind the changes that shrink-proofing brings, while others avoid these treated fibers.

Carbonizing is a method that removes VM from heavily contaminated fleeces. Scoured wool is exposed to acid and heat, and when very carefully monitored, the VM will be degraded faster than the wool fibers. The acid is then removed and the VM breaks down into dust, falling out of the fiber during further processing.

If worsted preparations are as aligned and straightened as possible, is the opposite a complete disarrangement of the fiber mass? Sometimes. But if a woolen preparation is defined as a loose, unorganized mass of fibers, then neither rolags nor rovings are truly woolen. Typically woolen preparations include a variety of fiber types (e.g., variations in staple length and sometimes micron count) and modifications in the orientation of the fibers as they meet the twist. Handcarded rolags are thought of as the perfect woolen preparation. However, skillful handcarding techniques do organize the fiber. If we make perfect rolags out of a perfectly consistent Cormo fleece, the fibers will be carefully arranged and organized. The fibers will all be the same length and have the same character. What makes this a woolen preparation then? The answer is in the spinning. As the rolag is spun from the end of the tube, the fibers in the rolag are oriented perpendicular to the direction in which the twist will enter the fibers. This orientation sends the fibers swirling around the point of twist, trapping air in the yarn. The result will be decidedly different than if the same fleece was combed or flicked. This is why handspinning is laden with never-ending, fascinating conversations about how seemingly simple theories work in practice. The many subtleties and nuances can make learning about handspinning more difficult, but the good news is that there is always something new to learn and ponder. The most experienced spinners I know are always learning and growing, so don't be afraid to ask questions.

Common Problems with Prepared Fibers

Many problem fibers can be improved or used in different ways.

Felting

Felting is often found in both roving and combed top preparations. In roving, it may occur when the fiber has been handled too many times or has been agitated—for example, the poor ball of roving that is left in the bottom of a spinner's bag for too long. The

Sometimes a felted roving can be drafted slightly or opened up before spinning.

more organized fibers of a combed top are a little more resistant to felting. Sometimes compacted fibers can be loosened by simply snapping a length of top or roving in the air. If you are working with combed top that is a bit felted, try opening the fibers width-wise to loosen them without changing the alignment. Many spinners predraft (drafting fibers along the length of the preparation). This step alters the preparation and color effect in handpainted fibers, so do a sample first if necessary.

Sticky Residue

Wool fibers can also have a sticky or tacky residue that makes drafting difficult. This can be caused when either a small amount of residual lanolin or carding oil added during processing dries out and oxidizes. This fiber can be carefully washed before it is spun, or it can be drafted a bit as for lightly felted fibers, spun, and then washed in hot water.

Washing Sticky Roving

Residue in roving can be caused by several things, some easier to remove than others. Try washing a small test piece first. Fill a sink with warm to hand-hot, soapy water. Place a small chunk of roving in the water for several minutes. Take the fiber out and repeat with warm rinse water. Allow to fully dry. If the roving is no longer sticky, the residue was likely carding oil added during processing, which is generally easy to remove with washing. If the roving is still sticky, the fiber will need to be scoured, and the residue is likely the natural lanolin and waxes produced by the sheep as the wool is growing. Scouring the roving does add an element of risk—the fibers could be felted in the process if you are not very careful. Weigh your options before scouring roving and be sure that removing

Roving being wrapped in tulle for washing.

Before washing (left) and after washing (right). The unwashed, sticky fibers are much more compacted.

Carded Merino wool with neps (left) and carded Corriedale wool with scurf (right).

residue is worth the risk and extra work. Remember—felting is forever! (See Chapter 2 for instructions on scouring.)

Debris—Neps, Noils, VM, Scurf

Processed fibers can have a number of unwanted materials included in the final preparation. Some of this debris, such as short fibers from shearing (second cuts), VM, and scurf, originates at the farm. Generally, the more processing the fleece undergoes, the more debris will be eliminated. However, processing can also sometimes cause broken fibers to tangle, creating neps and noils. In some mill situations, noils are to be expected when carding very fine fleeces, so the noils formed during carding are then removed by combing. If you have purchased roving that is noil-laden or has a large amount of VM, you can handcomb the fiber if you are determined to improve the preparation.

If a preparation has many short fibers but is spinning smoothly, the skeins can be fulled (lightly felted) to help secure short fibers and reduce pilling.

Custom Woolen Mills

What if you want to select your own fleece, but skip the preparation and go straight to spinning? You can send your own raw, skirted fleece off to the mill, and it will be returned to you clean and prepared. Some fibers are a better fit than others for mill processing, and results will be a bit different depending on the mill.

Here are some characteristics of fleeces that are best fit for custom mill processing:

Skirted and fairly clean. Depending on the equipment used for processing, a small to fairly large amount of debris can be removed, but the less you start with, the less you will end up with in the finished preparation. Some types of VM, such as burrs, are a particular problem and make processing difficult. Typically, the fleece-processing fee is based on weight—if you don't skirt a fleece, you are simply paying more for debris removal.

Strong and healthy. Check your fleece in several places for breaks and tender tips, as these fibers can be damaged during mechanical processing.

Moderate staple length. There is a certain amount of breakage during processing, so a very short starting staple length might be reduced even further. Long-staple fibers are more likely to be broken during processing. Many mills will not accept fleeces that are shorter than 2 inches (5 cm) or longer than 5 inches (12.5 cm).

Mill Tour

Depending on the mill you work with, you might have a number of fiber preparations to choose from. Each custom mill is unique, and

Picker at Zeilingers.

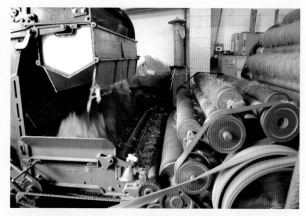
Picked fleece drops from the feedbox onto the first rotating drum.

As the fiber makes its way through the machine, it is carried along by several sets of stripper and worker drums.

The fiber comes off of the final drum in a wide, flat sheet called a web.

we spinners are very lucky that so many mills continue to exist. If you have questions about having your fleece processed, contact the mill for advice.

Here is a look around the Zeilinger Wool Company, which is a large custom mill in Frankenmuth, Michigan, with a variety of processing options. *Note: Not all woolen mills offer all of these services, and some types of mill equipment might look quite different, but the process is basically the same.*

Picking

After a fleece is washed and dried, it is fed into a picker. A mill-scale picker functions the same way as a home-scale picker but operates at a high rate of speed. The metal teeth catch the fleece and tease the fibers out of their natural lock formation. Loosening the fibers in the lock means less work for the carding machines. Some VM and debris will begin to fall out during picking. Some spinners choose picking as the final stage of processing, spinning straight from these teased locks. More

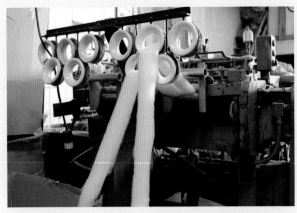

Several carded rovings are fed into the pin-drafter.

One pin-drafted roving emerges.

Many pin-drafted rovings are fed into the combing machine.

Metal combs separate the prime fiber from noils and debris.

often, though, this is an intermediate step that precedes carding.

An example of a good fleece for picking would be a nice 4-inch (10 cm) staple Border Leicester or Cotswold fleece. Some mills will also dye your fiber, so you could have several colors picked together. This would be a great fit for fiber that you want to spin into an airy, slightly textured yarn. Picking is also helpful if you want to process this kind of fleece into art batts using a drumcarder but don't want to do the washing, dyeing, and teasing.

Carding

Carding is the process during which the teased fiber is fully opened and formed into a continuous roving. The wool is dropped onto the first rotating drum, which is covered in carding cloth. As the wool is carried forward and passes between a series of drums moving at different rates, the fibers are attenuated and fully released from the lock. Depending on the mill setup, there may be several such machines, which are referred to as breakers. Once the fibers have reached the end of the carding process, they should be fully opened and somewhat aligned in a homogenous web. The term *web* refers to the smooth, flat sheet of fibers that spans the carding cloth, which is 60 inches (153 cm) wide at the Zeilinger mill. Some carders include peralta rollers, which are incredibly heavy metal cylinders that pulverize VM as the fiber passes between them. To create roving, the web is pulled off of the last drum, called a doffer.

Fleeces with a moderate fiber length, moderate crimp, and no breaks will stand up to the carding process beautifully. Zeilinger Wool Company processes quite a lot of American Shetland wool for breeders and fiber artists, and there can be huge differences in Shetland fleece types. The picking and carding process also helps to mix the fibers within a fleece into a more consistent blend.

Pin-Drafting

Pin-drafting machines can be used by mills to further process carded roving. Several rovings are fed into the pin-drafter at a time. As the rovings come together, the individual fibers are attenuated and pulled into closer alignment as they begin to form a more compact and consistent single roving. This preparation begins to look more like combed top because the fibers are beginning to be straightened and aligned as they move through the machine. What makes this process different from combed top is that none of the short fibers are removed and only a small amount of VM shakes loose. Pin-drafted roving is a great preparation for handspinning semiworsted yarns that are a balance of airy elasticity and smooth finish for good stitch definition.

Because pin-drafting does not remove short fibers or VM yet can yield a smooth preparation, very clean, strong fleeces are optimal. An ideal candidate might be a coated Corriedale fleece. One of the most beloved characteristics of Corriedale is its springy, bouncy crimp. Pin-drafting allows the crimp to remain active while keeping a springy fleece organized. Using a coated fleece not only ensures that there is very little VM but also reduces damage to the lock tips.

Combing

Each step of wool processing moves the fiber closer to smooth perfection. Combing is the step in which the longest and strongest fibers are separated from short fibers, tangles, and VM. What percentage of fiber makes it into the finished combed top and how much is waste or by-product depends greatly on the fiber used. A combing machine uses a series of rotating combs with fine teeth that pass through the fiber. The best fiber is pulled forward into a consistent web, which is slightly twisted as it exits the combing machine and is piled neatly into a canister.

Fine fleeces sustain more damage during the carding stage and are also more stubborn about releasing embedded VM than coarse fleeces. Delicate, fine fibers such as Cormo can be processed to best effect by going all the way through to the combing stage to remove the broken short fibers and VM. These buttery soft fleeces are a pleasure to spin when well prepared, but they can put up quite a struggle when the spinner is trying to manage fine fibers mixed with noils and chaff.

WORKING WITH WOOL:

Norwegian-Inspired Embroidered Mitts

A number of years ago, while happily buried deep inside a museum collection storeroom, I met a stunning pair of embroidered gloves from Norway. I was a spinner and a knitter and had done some embroidery. However, it wasn't until that moment that I realized I had never considered creating my own embroidered fabric made entirely of my own handspun. Such assumptions are not uncommon and are akin to the myth that handspun yarns cannot be used to warp a loom. Thus began my near-obsession with spinning, knitting, and embroidering Norwegian-inspired handcoverings.

In the latter half of the nineteenth century, textiles were changing rapidly with the introduction of synthetic dyes and the availability of millspun yarns. Looking closely at Norwegian handcoverings, we can see the balance of new and old traditions. Mittens (*votter*), gloves (*vanter*), and fingerless mitts (*pulsvanter*) were often knitted with woolen yarn and lightly felted to create a firm, long-wearing fabric. Embroidery could then be added to the backs of the hands and thumb gussets using brightly colored yarns and regional motifs. Ingebørg Gravjord explains in her wonderful book *Votten I Norsk Tradisjon (Mittens in the Norwegian Tradition)* that

embroidery yarns are an easy place to see the shift, starting in the mid-nineteenth century, from handspun, naturally dyed yarns using wool from Norwegian sheep to millspun yarns that were often imported in a vibrant range of synthetic colors.

A wide variety of woolen embroidery yarns can be seen when looking at Norwegian hand-coverings in museum collections. They range from two- to four-ply and from crisp, shiny yarns to bouncy, airy yarns—and sometimes multiple yarn types occur in one piece. All of these yarns, however, tend to be worsted-spun yarns. Worsted-spun yarns are durable and work into embroidered motifs with clear edges and distinct stitches. Today, we can spin a wide range of embroidery yarns in as many colors as we can imagine.

Spinning

This project is a great way to see how different fiber preparations and spinning styles interact. Since the mitts themselves are fulled, a preparation that is on the woolen end of the continuum works well. This can range from carded rolags to some types of commercial combed top preparations that incorporate a wide variety of staple lengths. Traditionally,

Bright millspun embroidery yarns were widely available by the close of the nineteenth century. These mitts (VM.1968.028.001) were brought to the United States by Borghild Halvorson from Hallingdal in about 1907. Vesterheim Norwegian-American Museum, Decorah, Iowa.

combed tops contained fibers that were all the same length, but many commercial tops are made today from a variety of fiber types and staple lengths. Blends of fibers, such as Merino and yak, and some types of wools, such as Shetland, can incorporate fibers of different lengths. When these fibers are spun with a worsted draw, the yarn will have the strength of a worsted yarn, but the short fibers will add a lofty, woolen effect. When these yarns are knitted and lightly fulled, the short fibers will bloom a bit, thickening the fabric and creating a smooth surface for embroidery, as well as a warm pair of mitts.

Worsted embroidery yarns tend to work best. They are strong and smooth enough to withstand the embroidery process and durable enough to wear well on the surface of the textile. When deciding how much twist to add, keep in mind that there is a fine balance between durability and loft. Spinning these fine embroidery yarns with moderate twist makes them more fragile than high-twist yarns, but they will have more loft and less distinct plies, giving the finished piece a flat, even appearance. This works especially well for embroidery motifs that use satin stitch to fill in large areas.

For motifs that use chain-, stem-, or cross-stitching, a firm, higher-twist yarn works great. Does your pattern use all of these? Try using more than one type of yarn in your work.

Fulling

Finishing these mitts by lightly felting them, a process called fulling, tightens the stitches a bit and thickens the fabric. Fulling encourages the fibers to bloom and fill the spaces between stitches, making these mitts warm and creating a smooth surface to apply embroidery.

I full my handcoverings in the sink with warm to hot water and a little soap. I suggest weaving in the loose ends and turning the gloves inside out for best results. Begin rubbing the gloves between your hands in the hot, slightly soapy water. Work each finger and thumb and make sure to rub the fabric in multiple directions for even fulling. Rinse under cold water and roll in a towel. Block and allow to dry completely before embroidering.

Embroidery

Embroidering on a knitted surface can be more challenging than on a woven one, but there are a few tricks to make it easier. Cut a piece of thin cardboard so it will slip inside the glove, providing a smooth working surface and separating the front and back of the glove. The cardboard should hold the glove taut but not stretch the fabric. This will prevent the knitted fabric from puckering in addition to keeping the embroidery stitches on the back of the hand to avoid accidentally sewing back and front together.

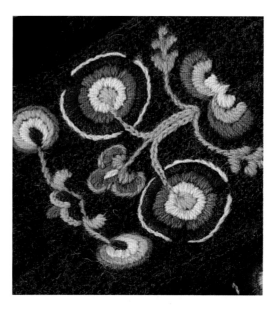

While many of the extant nineteenth-century handcoverings from Norway appear to have been embroidered freehand (without a pattern on the surface of the work) and many modern embroiderers also prefer to work in this way, we can use water-soluble stabilizer or waste canvas to apply a pattern. Trace the embroidery motif onto the clear stabilizer with a marker and baste the stabilizer to the glove with sewing thread. Place the stabilizer face down on the glove to ensure that the marker will not rub off as you handle the work. After embroidery is applied, soak the piece in warm water to dissolve the stabilizer and shape the gloves to dry.

Spinning Wool

4

Yarn /yärn/ 1: A spun thread used for knitting, weaving, or sewing. 2: A long or rambling story.

The yarn that connects us with spinners of the past is, indeed, long and rambling. Wool and twist and human hands created yarns that were woven into Viking sailcloth and the fine threads of the Bayeux Tapestry just as we today can make colorful modern yarns with the same elemental ingredients. Adding twist to fiber creates yarn—handspinning is as simple as that and yet complex enough to captivate the interest of many spinners for a lifetime.

Woolen & Worsted —A Continuum

Woolen and worsted are terms that refer to fiber preparations, and they are also used to describe spinning methods, known as drafting techniques. **Draft** refers to the way in which the fibers are attenuated (stretched out) and manipulated as they are spun into yarn. With different combinations of fiber preparation and drafting methods, spinners can create yarns with very different qualities that range from airy and bouncy to smooth and shiny, with many exciting yarns in between. How different yarn types interrelate is a source of infinite conversations among handspinners, but a simple approach is to think about handspun yarns as a continuum of yarn types with smooth, dense worsted yarns on one end, and lofty woolen yarns on the other. Understanding the extremes can help you find where other yarns fit in the range of yarn possibilities.

Worsted Spinning

Spinning worsted-style is how many spinners first learn to make yarn because it is the method that often lets the spinner feel more in control. Like worsted preparation, worsted spinning takes its name from the English town of Worstead, famous for its smooth, fine, woven cloth since the Middle Ages (see A History of Worsted in Worstead, page 66). Today, combed fibers for worsted spinning are more readily available than ever, or you can join in the long Worstead tradition and prepare your own.

For a classic worsted yarn, start with a combed preparation of a wool that is longer than 3½ inches (9 cm), preferably of a wool with low crimp, such as Leicester, Romney, or Lincoln. When these fibers are combed, the fibers are all oriented in the same direction as the yarn. If the fibers are drafted and attenuated (stretched out) as the twist enters, the crimp is subdued and the yarn will be as smooth and firm as possible. Essentially, as much air as

WOOLEN VS WORSTED SPINNING

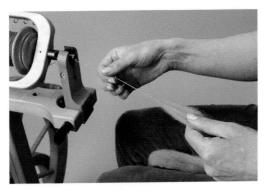 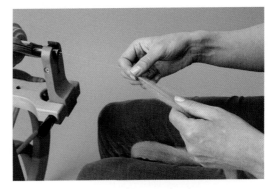

The difference between woolen and worsted spinning in practice comes down to this: a woolen draw (left) is spinning in the presence of twist, while a worsted draw (right) is spinning in the absence of twist.

WORSTED SPINNING

Worsted yarn, commercial and handcombed tops, and handcomb.

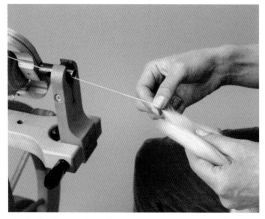

Pinch the fibers where the twist enters the unspun fibers.

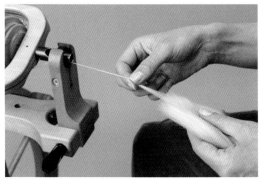

Draw the fibers forward, attenuating them toward the wheel or spindle, until about two-thirds of the staple length is between your pinching fingers and the fiber supply. Take note of where the fibers seem to be moving out of the combed top.

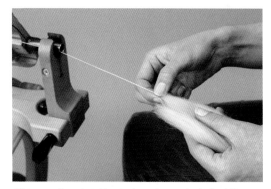

Slide your front hand back along the newly drafted fibers, but don't let the twist come between your hands. Stop at the point where the fibers were moving out of the fiber supply. Now you can draft forward again to repeat the process.

possible has been pushed out. I usually prefer a short forward draft toward the wheel when I spin with a worsted draw, but some spinners prefer to draft away from the wheel. Try it and see what you like best. On a spindle, fibers can be held and drafted horizontally or vertically.

As you practice and explore different types of fibers, you can experiment with how far the fibers are drafted forward and where your fingers stop moving back. The fewer fibers you draft forward, the finer your yarn will be, and the more fibers you draft forward, the thicker your yarn will be.

Spinning across the top, or spinning off the tips as it is sometimes called, is a technique that builds upon basic worsted spinning and allows the spinner to easily control a large fiber supply. Commercial combed tops can be quite bulky, and keeping the twist moving steadily across the entire mass will prevent the top from becoming disorganized, with the

WORSTED SPINNING, CONTINUED

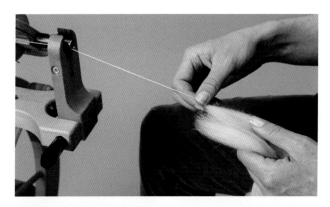

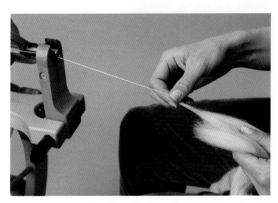
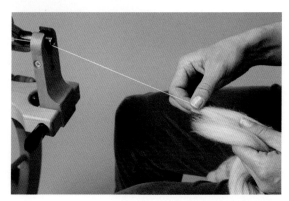

Some spinners prefer a short, backward worsted draw, in which your fiber hand would move away from the point of twist for a distance of about two-thirds of the staple length before your pinching fingers allow the twist to enter the newly drafted fibers.

118

WORSTED SPINNING WITH A SPINDLE

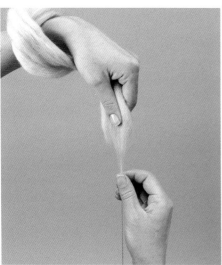 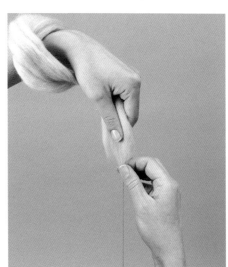

Worsted spinning on a spindle is the same as on a wheel. Pinch the fibers where the twist enters the fibers, draft forward, and then slide your fingers along the newly drafted fibers to insert the twist. When using a spindle, you can draft vertically as shown with one hand over the other, or horizontally with hands side by side.

SPINNING ACROSS THE TOP

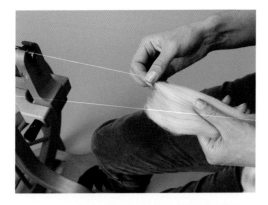

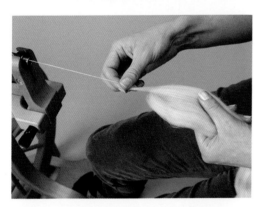

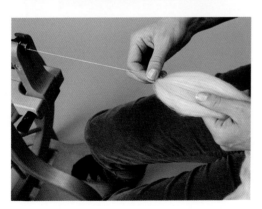

fiber spun along one edge and the remaining fiber a messy bundle. We have all been there! Spinning across the top also comes in handy when spinning marled yarns with several colors held and spun simultaneously.

Give it a try: With a short forward draw, attenuate the fibers and slide your fingers (and the twist) back toward the fiber supply again but slightly offset from where the previous fibers were spun. Repeat this short forward draw, moving back and forth across the exposed edge of the fibers. I have met many spinners who only like to move one direction or another across the top. No problem! If you feel comfortable moving from right to left but not returning, just turn the fiber over and continue working as before. With some practice, this technique is an incredibly valuable tool for spinning beautiful worsted yarns.

Troubleshooting Worsted Spinning

Here are some suggestions for dealing with issues that might come up during worsted spinning.

Fiber Too Short for Worsted Spinning

In order for a worsted draw to work well, the fibers must be long enough to draw forward (or backward) about two-thirds of the staple length and allow the twist to enter the attenuated fibers. For fibers shorter than about 3 inches (7.5 cm), this can be difficult. For fibers shorter than 2 inches (5 cm), try a semiwoolen draw for a firmer yarn and a woolen draw for a softer yarn.

Splitting Combed Tops

There are many strong opinions in the handspinning community about splitting commercial combed tops. My personal belief is that every technique we come into contact with is a useful tool that might be just right in a certain situation. However, it is important to understand that this is a technique that changes our fiber preparation. Here are two hypothetical responses from two hypothetical spinners.

Anti-splitting: This fiber was processed and combed and handled with care to produce a perfect preparation. Why ruin it by disarranging the fibers? Better spinning habits, such as learning to spin across the top, can correct any problems you are having.

Pro-splitting: Sometimes, commercial combed tops can be quite large. When spinning in a dry climate or during the winter, static electricity can make these fibers flare at the tips and not stay nicely arranged. I feel more comfortable managing fewer fibers at one time. It makes me happy.

My opinion is that spinning a perfect, pristine combed top without splitting is ideal. However, if managing less fiber at a time is more comfortable for you, the spinning police will not carry you away. Splitting is especially useful when spinning handpainted tops to manage color changes or to loosen compacted or slightly felted preparations. It is important to understand that splitting a combed top permanently alters color repeats and fiber preparation.

Here are some tips for safer splitting:

Start splitting a few inches below the tips. Split upward and then continue down. The tips will

SPLITTING A COMBED TOP

Split the top just below the tips of the fiber.

Begin separating the top, splitting down the length of the fibers. Moving your hands down to the point of separation every few inches as you gently pull the top apart will keep the fibers more organized.

be tidier and the split placement can be more easily controlled.

Know your staple length. Hold the top firmly and draw apart about a staple length at a time, keeping your hands close to where the fiber is splitting to control the fibers and cause the least amount of disruption to the combed top.

Slubs, Oh My!

Slubs, or thick spots in your yarn, can happen during worsted spinning for several reasons. The first thing to check is the staple length of the fiber you are working with. If you are drafting forward or backward more than the staple length, you will get a slub in the yarn. Slub yarns can be fun to make, but if you are looking for a consistent yarn, try drafting about two-thirds of the staple length.

Slubs can also happen when our pinching fingers move too far into the unspun fibers. Try watching where the fibers move out of the combed top, and keep your fingers closer to this area.

My Beautiful Fiber Is Now a Sweaty Wad of Stuff

When spinning preparations in which all the fibers are straight and aligned, as in combed top or combed locks, it is easy to have the twist move down the side of the fiber prep instead of moving back and forth along the top. Take care to spin on the tips: moving your fingers back and forth along the top will help. If the yarn starts to eat down the side of the fiber, simply break the yarn and bring it back up to the tips and rejoin.

Difficult Drafting

In worsted spinning, the hand closest to the wheel is the most active, and it's easy to lose track of what the other hand, the fiber-supply hand, is doing. If this hand holds the fiber supply too tightly, or if the thumb presses the fiber too firmly, fibers will have trouble moving forward as they are drafted into the yarn. Relax—your fibers and hands and yarn will benefit. Also remember that the fiber itself could be creating an extra challenge. (See Common Problems with Prepared Fibers, page 104.)

Slubs can be repeated intentionally to create textured yarns, but are less desirable when spinning a smooth, consistent yarn.

Woolen Spinning

Woolen-type yarns are created when twist enters loose fibers. Because the fibers are not smoothed or straightened as they are twisted, they create more air pockets, resulting in a lightweight yarn with lots of loft and a fuzzy surface. This fuzzy surface causes woolen yarns to be less reflective, and often softer to the touch, than their smooth, worsted cousins. Woolen yarns can also be more prone to pilling, depending on how the yarn was finished and used.

To spin a true woolen yarn, the fibers need to be 3½ inches (9 cm) or shorter in staple length and carded into a classic rolag. Why? Handcarding will align the fibers to a greater degree, and when they are rolled into a little tube from the top of the card toward the handle, the fibers are now oriented perpendicular to the tube. This means that when the rolag is spun from one end of the tube, the fibers will be presented sideways as the twist enters. The fibers will swirl around as the twist enters, creating those important air spaces that make woolen yarns so warm. This also means that there are more fibers poking out the side of the yarn, giving the surface a classic woolly look (see illustration on page 65).

Learning to spin with a woolen long draw can often leave spinners feeling as if they have limited control over the size and consistency of the yarn. This is partly the nature of the technique and fiber preparation used, but it also has to do with the way in which twist is managed during woolen spinning.

The gauge of a woolen-spun yarn is determined by the force of the twist as it enters the fiber supply. The more twist, the larger the yarn, and vice versa. When using a supported long draw technique (one of several types of woolen draws), the forward hand can also manage how much twist enters the drafting zone. The gauge of the yarn is primarily determined by how much twist is allowed into the drafting zone and how fast the fiber-supply hand attenuates the fibers by moving away from the point of twist. When I was learning to spin long draw, breaking the process into three steps was helpful: pinch the yarn with the forward hand near the wheel or spindle, draft back several inches with the fiber-supply hand, release the forward hand's pinch to allow twist to enter the yarn.

To spin with a supported woolen long draw, keep your forward hand close to the wheel and don't be tempted to move it to where the twist is entering the fibers. This forward hand pinches the yarn gently as the fiber hand draws away from the point of twist. The forward hand then releases to allow twist to enter the newly drafted fibers. Once the fiber hand has moved back as far as is comfortable, allow the yarn to enter the wheel orifice and wind onto the bobbin, in one long motion—or long draw.

WOOLEN SPINNING

Pinch the yarn with the forward hand near the wheel or spindle.

Draft back several inches with the fiber-supply hand.

Release the forward hand's pinch to allow twist to enter the yarn.

WOOLEN SPINNING WITH A SPINDLE

Woolen spinning on a spindle is the same as on a wheel. Pinch the yarn with the forward hand near the spindle, move the back hand away from the point of twist, and release the forward hand to allow the twist to enter the yarn between your hands.

Troubleshooting Woolen Spinning

Here are some suggestions for dealing with issues that might come up during woolen spinning.

I Can't Draft

If the twist is entering the fiber supply too aggressively, you will no longer be able to draft the fiber. This can be adjusted in several ways. Either move your fiber hand away from the point of twist more quickly, or change to a slower (larger) pulley. You can also increase the take-up tension on your spinning wheel so the yarn is pulled onto the bobbin faster.

My Yarn Keeps Breaking

If the twist is entering the fiber too slowly, the yarn will start to drift apart and break. This can be remedied by either moving your fiber-supply hand away from the point of twist more slowly, or if spinning on a wheel, change to a faster (smaller) pulley. This might also mean that you need to reduce the take-up tension on your wheel. As you are spinning, make sure that your forward hand is allowing twist to enter the area between your hands.

Difficult Drafting

Woolen-style spinning usually works best with fibers that are 3½ inches (9 cm) and shorter. When working with longer-staple fibers, you might find that the twist quickly enters the drafting zone and locks the fibers in place before you can easily draft. Let's say you are working with perfectly prepared Lincoln top. These fibers would be low crimp, longer than 3½ inches, and smoothly aligned. One solution is to spin from the fold. Fold a staple-length bundle of fiber over the first finger of your fiber hand. Join the yarn to the bundle by allowing the twist to enter the bundle in the center of the fibers, and begin spinning with a woolen draw.

Another reason it might be difficult to draft is if the wheel is inserting twist into the yarn faster than drafting is occurring. Try changing to a larger pulley or increasing the take-up tension. Drafting shouldn't be difficult. If it is, there might be something about the fiber that is creating an extra challenge. (See Common Problems with Prepared Fibers, page 104.)

Semiwoolen, Semiworsted, Semi-Something...

What happens if a woolen preparation, such as a rolag, is spun with a worsted draw? Semiwoolen and semiworsted are terms given to the many yarns that fall somewhere between woolen and worsted because they combine elements of both. Understanding the difference between the two can be confusing because spinners and well-respected spinning instructors often use the two terms in very different ways. I like to define semiwoolen yarns versus semiworsted yarns based on how the fibers are drafted and how the twist is inserted, rather than on the method of fiber preparation.

Semiwoolen

The yarns that fall in the semiwoolen category are spun in the presence of twist, meaning the twist is between your hands. Whether the result is more woolen-like or worsted-like mostly depends on the staple length of the fibers. Short fibers will yield a more woolen-type yarn, while long fibers will straighten out and behave more like a worsted yarn.

Allow the twist to enter the drafting zone between your forward hand and fiber hand. By using a short forward draw, you can create a yarn that has a more woolen surface but the strength of a worsted yarn. This method works especially well for fibers that are fairly short but will be used in a textile needing some additional strength and density.

Semiworsted

Semiworsted yarns are often made by combining a woolen-style preparation with worsted-style spinning. Because the fibers in the woolen preparation are disarranged, this yarn can never be as smooth as a true worsted yarn, but it can still be spun into a durable and hard-wearing yarn. There are many traditional examples of semiworsted yarns spun and used throughout northern Europe.

Another yarn that often falls into the semiworsted category is one that is spun worsted but contains fibers that vary in length. A great example would be a blend of 50 percent Merino, 50 percent baby camel down. This scrumptious blend is readily available as a combed top preparation and spins easily with a worsted drafting method. Worsted preparation plus worsted spinning should equal a worsted yarn, right? Not exactly. The camel down fibers are much shorter than the Merino fibers, so unless the yarn has very high twist, these short, fine fibers will be less confined and arranged than in a true worsted yarn. Once the finished skein has been washed, the camel fibers will bloom and give the yarn a soft halo. Yarns like these can yield the best of both worlds—the strength and consistency of a worsted yarn, with the soft finish of a woolen yarn.

The yarns described here are only the very tip of the spinning iceberg. There are endless combinations of fibers, preparations, and drafting techniques, creating fodder for equally endless conversations among spinners. You can learn more from other books and resources and from other spinners on social media sites such as Ravelry. However, the most important teacher is practice. Challenge your assumptions, try new techniques, and above all, spin!

SEMIWOOLEN SPINNING

With your forward hand, pinch the yarn several inches above the point of twist.

Forward hand drafts the fiber toward the wheel or spindle as for worsted draw (about ²/₃ of the staple length of the fiber).

The forward hand realeases and repeats the draft again.

Plying

Plying is twisting two or more singles together. Typically, during the plying step, twist is added in the direction opposite the one in which the singles were spun, removing much of the twist in the singles. This allows the fiber to regain loft and bounce, while the plied structure adds strength and durability. Handspun yarns will often be improved by incorporating plying into the yarn design, but there are also textiles that work best with a singles yarn.

Getting Ready to Ply

So now the bobbin is full of beautiful singles—what happens next? From many wonderful encounters with spinners in my textile travels, I know that there are countless strategies for handling singles when spinning for a project. In my early spinning days, I would spin two bobbins of singles and then ply those two bobbins together to make a two-ply yarn (or three bobbins to make a three-ply yarn). I was quite happy with the yarns that I spun this way; however, when plying several skeins for a project, the first skein differed enough from the last one that I could see the change in my finished garments. Spinning all of the singles needed for a project before beginning to ply allows the singles to be mixed together, first and last, as they are plied into skeins. This gives the most consistent group of skeins possible and can greatly improve large projects that require multiple skeins, such as cozy knitted sweaters and finely woven shawls.

Another technique I use to increase consistency and handle yarns easily is to rewind my singles from the wheel onto storage bobbins. This extra step attenuates the yarn over a distance (try keeping your wheel and full bobbin at least 10 feet from the bobbin winder), allowing the twist to even out. Imagine the spot where you slowed your drafting to pick out a noil, overtwisting the yarn—the extra twist spreads out into neighboring yards as the yarn is rewound. The change is subtle, but I can see its impact in my own work. This also allows me to keep all of my singles on storage bobbins before plying, rather than filling up expensive spinning-wheel bobbins.

There are many approaches to plying, but the method shown here requires one hand to be in constant movement and one hand to remain stationary. The hand that typically holds the fiber supply will be stationary, somewhere near your lap, and will be separating and tensioning the yarns that stretch from the bobbins on the lazy kate. The forward hand pinches the point of twist and can also separate the yarns under tension. By pinching the point of twist while the singles are held under tension, the twist can be guided into place as the singles untwist slightly and settle together. Begin treadling with the wheel moving in the opposite direction as it did when the singles were spun and allow the forward hand to move slowly toward the fiber hand. The forward hand then moves toward the wheel, allowing the newly plied yarn to wind onto the bobbin. This hand remains in steady, constant motion. It can be helpful, especially when plying a large project, to count how many treadles this movement takes.

How Much Ply Twist?

Many spinners use a piece of self-plied yarn to see how much ply twist will be needed. As you are spinning singles, simply take a length of singles yarn and fold it in half, allowing it to ply on itself. Tie a knot in the end, and then use it as a guide when plying. This control sample can be compared to the yarn during plying to help keep the ply twist consistent. There are a couple of limitations to this practice, though. As singles sit on a bobbin, the twist will go dormant. Then, if stale singles are folded back on themselves, they will not look at all like the control self-ply sample made when the singles were first spun. In addition, the control sample

---

To Ply or Not to Ply

Singles yarns can never be described as balanced yarns. They are, by their very nature, unbalanced. The twist is added in only one direction, and the fibers will be laboring to right themselves. These yarns can be "energized" and used to intentionally change the surface of a finished textile; they can be moderately twisted, adding just enough twist to hold the yarn together but not bias the work; or they can be fulled after spinning to add stability to the yarn and neutralize the active twist.

I designed the Among the Birches cowl (page 140) to make good use of fulled singles.

The inaptly named lazy kate is an essential spinner's tool. Some wheels come with built-in kates, but for certain plying projects, a separate kate can be easier to use. A simple shoe-box kate (far right) with knitting needles to hold the bobbins works quite well.

PLYING

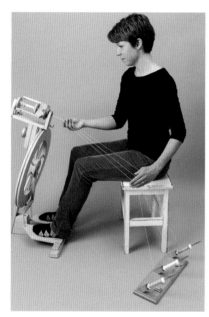
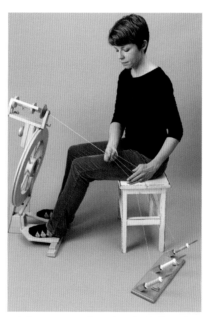
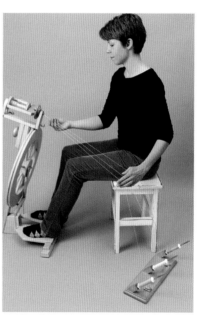

Placing the lazy kate and bobbins a good distance away from the wheel allows the twist to continue to move and even out in the singles before it is fixed in place during plying. For most projects, I don't use a tensioned lazy kate. If hand movements are smooth and intentional, the bobbins shouldn't spin out of control, causing tangles. When might a tensioned kate be handy? With plying techniques that require more manipulation, such as chain plying, or when plying high-twist yarns.

is of limited use when it comes to woolen-spun yarn in particular because very soft, airy singles may often be plied with extra ply twist to add strength and durability.

Splicing

The plying process also allows you to fix mistakes. If you encounter a particularly lumpy join or a fragile, thin spot in the singles, simply break the singles and remove the undesirable bit. A simple splice will rejoin the singles. Also use a splice to join in a new bobbin of singles when one runs out.

To splice: Stop plying several inches from the end of the broken ply. Lay in the new ply and allow the twist to enter the intact plies and the two ends of the broken ply. After the twist has entered, give the new ply a tug, allowing the end to tuck down into the yarn—and off you go!

Just a Few of the Ply Structures That Make Woolen Yarns Sing

Most spinners that I know spin singles to the right (called a Z-twist) and ply to the left (S-twist). However, all of the ply structures shown here can be reversed.

Plied yarns become rounder as more plies are added. The way in which these yarns behave when worked into a textile will vary. In a knitted fabric, three-ply yarns work well for things such as socks because, like a tripod, three plies are very stable and don't shift much as the fabric moves. Yarns with four plies don't have a natural center and are more supple in a moderate-twist yarn. These yarns work well for densely knitted work such as traditional Norwegian sweaters because the yarn folds more easily into a stitch and can be knitted with less strain on the knitter's hands—a very good thing.

> ### *Plying on a Spindle*
>
> Managing yarn for plying on a spindle can be done in the same way it is on a wheel. Many spinners use special lazy kates made to hold spindles or use a shoe-box kate to hold several spindles filled with singles for plying. Other spindle spinners choose to wind singles into a plying ball. Here's how it works: If you are planning a two-ply yarn, spin two groups of singles (either on different spindles or wound off the same spindle). Holding the ends of both singles, wind them together as a pair into a ball or center-pull ball. Now you are ready to insert the twist (in the opposite direction the singles were spun in most cases) and create a plied yarn.
>
> #### Keep Reading
>
> To learn more about spindles and the many ways in which they are used, check out Abby Franquemont's important book *Respect the Spindle.*

Z   **S**

Twist direction is often described as Z-twist (right twist) and S-twist (left twist). See how the angle of the yarns' plies aligns with the shape of the letters?

PLY STRUCTURES

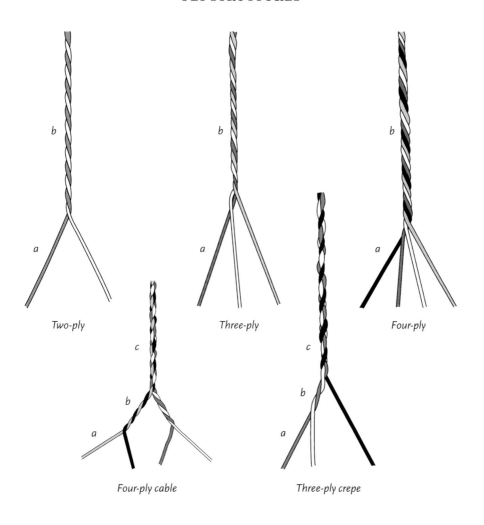

Two-ply

Three-ply

Four-ply

Four-ply cable

Three-ply crepe

Two-Ply

This is the simplest plying structure, and these supple yarns work especially well for weaving, knitted lace, embroidery, and more. Start with two singles (a) that were spun Z. Hold them together as the wheel or spindle is turning in the opposite direction, inserting S twist to create a two-ply yarn (b).

Three-Ply

These round, stable yarns tend to offer a nice balance of woolly loft and durability, making this a great workhorse yarn for knitters. Holding three singles (a) that were spun Z, ply them together by adding S-twist to make a three-ply yarn (b).

Four-Ply Yarn

Four plies spun together don't lock into place naturally like three plies, so the resulting yarn can be a bit more limber and lithe—great for colorwork knitting and plump crochet stitches. Starting with four singles (a) that were spun Z, ply all four together at once by adding S-twist to make a four-ply yarn (b).

Four-Ply Cable

Cable yarns have an almost woven look to their surfaces. While they can be bouncy and airy, they are surprisingly durable. Begin with two Z-spun singles (a) and ply them S with about twice as much ply twist as usual. Repeat this step with two more singles so you have two over-plied two-ply yarns (b). Both two-ply yarns are plied together Z, the same direction the singles were initially spun, to make a cabled yarn (c).

Three-Ply Crepe

These yarns have a single ply that wraps around a two-ply in the opposite direction. So, you will need two singles spun Z and one single that is spun S. All three plies can be similar in gauge to give a smooth, more traditional yarn, or all three can be different for textured effects. Start with two Z-spun singles (a) and ply them S with about twice as much ply twist as usual, creating an over-plied two-ply yarn (b). This two-ply yarn is then plied Z with an S-spun single to create a three-ply crepe yarn (c).

Finishing Yarns

After the yarn has made its final pass through the wheel or spindle, it needs to be finished. While there are multiple approaches to finishing woolen yarns, this step typically involves washing. A hot soak will relax twist, enliven the crimp, and leave your yarn feeling fresh and clean.

How yarn is handled when unwound from the bobbin or spindle cop will depend on its intended use. Most of the time, the first step is to wind the yarn into a skein. While an elbow is all that you need to create a skein of yarn, a niddy-noddy is a simple tool spinners use to measure yardage while creating a skein.

Using a Niddy-Noddy

Follow these steps to create a skein of yarn with a niddy-noddy.

1. Loosen or remove the band on the bobbin so it can rotate more freely on the wheel.

2. Hold the end of the yarn in the same hand that grasps the middle of the niddy-noddy.

3. Begin winding the yarn around the arms of the niddy-noddy, taking care as you go over and under the arms so that the yarn never crosses. You should be forming a continuous loop, folded in half.

4. Tie the skein in at least two places and slide the skein off one of the arms to remove.

WINDING A SKEIN WITH A NIDDY-NODDY

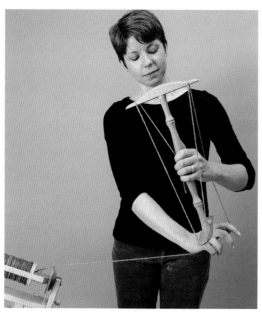
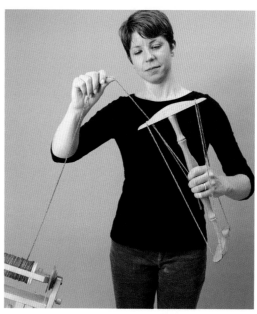

Tying a Skein

A common saying among spinners is that wool is "forgiving," and this is certainly true. Its elasticity and tendency to grab onto itself make it easy to handle and store. There are many great strategies for tying skeins, and I have outlined two of my favorites here.

Strategy 1: Tie each cut end of the skein in a quick half hitch to self-tie the skein in two places. This tie is as quick and easy to create as it is to remove later, but if the skein is to be dyed or fulled, it will need to be tied more securely.

Strategy 2: The cut ends of the skein are tied together into a knot. Then the skein is loosely,

TYING A SKEIN, STRATEGY 1

TYING A SKEIN, STRATEGY 2

yet securely tied with a figure-eight knot in four or more places with scrap yarn. If the ties are too tight, they can inhibit fulling or dye penetration in those areas.

Steam-Setting Skeins

Steam can be used to finish handspun yarns. Carding oils, residue, or excess dye will not be removed from the yarn, but the twist can be set by steaming. Spinners sometimes use this method to finish textured yarns, such as tailspun skeins that incorporate locks or other elements that could be altered if washed.

A Good Wash Does Wonders

Finishing is a term that usually refers to washing. Handspun yarns are finished in a variety of ways for different purposes. Yarns that are to be directly woven into cloth (not dyed first) are traditionally not washed but are finished once the cloth is woven, allowing the yarn and weave structure to interact. Yarns destined for knitting, crochet, or embroidery are typically finished before being worked into a completed textile.

Why wash your yarn? One reason is that if you have used commercially prepared fibers such as combed tops and rovings—from mills large and small—the fiber has been through a long journey before it came to rest, plied and waiting, on your bobbin. A good wash will remove any carding oil residue that was added during processing in the mill to protect the fiber and reduce static. Even for fleeces that you have washed and prepared yourself, a good wash can remove remaining dust and dirt from the farm.

Wet-finishing handspun yarns also gives the fibers a chance to move within the structure of the yarn, balancing and dispersing some of the twist added during spinning. This is often referred to by spinners as *setting the*

Spun in the Grease

There are many examples of traditional yarns that were, and still are, spun in the grease. Many of these yarns were washed *after* spinning, often in combination with dyeing. When washed, rather than scoured, these yarns retain lanolin in the core of the yarn.

As you can see, the washed skein (left) is much fuller than the unwashed one (right).

twist. When fibers are processed and spun, the natural crimp has been smoothed and subdued to varying degrees (and in the case of superwash fibers, permanently altered). The effect washing has on yarns depends on the particular combination of fiber preparation, yarn structure, and wool type. The washed and dried skeins will usually have more bounce and coherence (the plies will fit together more naturally) and can be noticeably shorter. Take time to measure your skeins after they are washed and dried to get an accurate yardage estimate.

There are three common methods of wet-finishing handspun yarns: washing, fulling, and blocking. To truly understand the art of finishing, sample many different combinations of yarn types and finishing methods. There are as many different ways to approach finishing as there are types of yarn. With that being said, a basic approach is that worsted-type yarns do well with a simple wash, woolen-type yarns bloom and balance when fulled, and unruly singles yarns and yarns with complex structures benefit from blocking.

Washing Your Handspun Yarns

Step 1. Fill a basin with warm to hot water and a bit of detergent. The detergent not only helps to remove remaining residues but also acts as a surfactant. Surfactants are wetting agents that break the surface tension of the water, allowing water molecules to make their way to the fiber surface faster.

For this washing step, I like to use something with a fragrance to mask the smell of the wool, which moths love. I use Kookaburra wool wash, Dawn dish detergent, or other similar products. Add skeins that can comfortably soak side by side with plenty of room. You can give the skeins a squeeze to help the water absorb, but don't agitate them too much or you will risk felting. Leave the skeins to soak for about 10 minutes.

Step 2. Remove the soapy skeins and squeeze the water out. Do not wring. Refill the basin with the same temperature water to rinse. Rinse just as if you were repeating the washing step minus the detergent. All washes and rinses should be done with nearly the same temperature water.

Step 3. Roll the skeins in a towel to remove excess water. Open up each skein and give it a

quick snap. This snap will help realign the fibers after washing. Hang the skeins and allow them to dry completely.

Fulled and Lightly Felted Finishes

Adding agitation to the washing step causes the fibers to move within the yarn structure to a greater degree, leaving the yarn with a fuzzy halo. For woolen-spun yarns in particular, this can add durability and consistency. Crimpy wools and short fibers that would be more likely to pill are opened up and secured in place, depending on the extent of the fulling process. Some spinners use a temperature change to help add a lightly felted finish to their handspun yarn. Be careful—if agitation is prolonged, a beautiful skein can become a solid, felted object. Quick samples will help guide you on how much fulling your yarn requires.

Step 1. Fill a basin of hot water and a second basin of cold water—or have a running cold-water tap handy. Add a small amount of detergent to the hot-water basin. (Wear rubber gloves if your hands are heat sensitive.)

Step 2. Place a skein in the hot, soapy water and agitate it with your hands. Squeeze out the excess water, submerge the skein in cold water, and squeeze as before. By repeating this process, the skein will be more intensely fulled. Fine wools such as Merino or Cormo will full quickly, while others might take more work. For moderate fulling, stop when the fibers in the yarn begin to stick together. If fulling a group of skeins for a project, keep track of how many hot and cold soaks each skein receives for consistency.

Step 3. Roll the skeins in a towel to remove excess water. Skeins finished this way can also be firmly smacked on a hard surface to help the fuzzy halo develop further. Don't be shy—hold one end of the skein and give it a swing, bringing it down quickly against a smooth, hard surface. Turn the skein around and repeat for the other end. Hang the skeins and allow them to dry completely.

Blocking

Woolen yarns and textiles have a special elasticity thanks to wool's inherent crimp. This allows wool fibers to be lightly stretched and still return to their natural shape. Just how far a wool fiber can be stretched without damage depends on the crimp character. Blocking is a process in which wool is stretched or formed into a desired shape, and through the addition of water or steam, the wool fibers will retain some of this shape after the wool is dry. Yarn can be blocked in the skein, or textiles such as knitted lace can be blocked after the piece is completed. There are good reasons to block skeins, but keep in mind that lightly blocked skeins will regain some of their natural shape and could alter a textile after it has been created.

Sampling: Quick and Consistent

Sampling, swatching, and other assorted acts of preplanning are useful tools when it comes to intentional spinning. Handspun yarns can be subtley changed in innumerable ways by the choices made throughout the yarn-making process: drafting techniques, singles twist versus ply twist, finishing, and more. The impact of all of these choices on how the final yarn looks and feels isn't a sure thing until it is washed and fully dried. When spinning for a particular project, be it embroidery, knitting, or crochet, a swatch of the pattern that has been washed and fully dried is the best way to know how the yarn will behave in the final textile.

To Plan or Not to Plan . . .

Never an absolutist, I always keep a place in my work for projects in which the planning process never interrupts the creative flow. I love the indulgence of diving into a project head first at 2 a.m. with an artist's abandon. Spinning for the pure pleasure of feeling fiber under your fingertips doesn't require grist calculations or note-taking. If the act of spinning takes precedence over the exactness of the final yarn, just jump in and find your bliss!

There are many ways to measure and record the yarns we create—and the most important aspect of record-keeping is in actually remembering to do it!

For many spinners, acquiring a deep affection for sampling can take some time. Finding a system for creating consistent samples that fit your learning style is important. For me, it was important that sampling and record-keeping kept pace with my creative flow. But developing a balanced relationship between organization and creativity, without allowing either to limit the other, can be a challenge. The following is a method I have developed over the years to help me create quick, consistent samples that give me the information I need to anticipate how a project will turn out before I start. Sampling allows for an evolution of ideas, and I see my work improve through the process.

Kate's Creative Process

I start with a fiber and a general idea about yarn design. Let's say I am going to sample a worsted-spun three-ply yarn. I first spin a few yards to see how the fiber feels at a particular tension and drive ratio. Once I have settled in, I insert a piece of scrap fiber into the fiber supply to mark the beginning of my sample. I don't use the first few yards in my sample because my spinning is the least consistent in the first few yards of a new bobbin. For my three-ply sample, I will spin three small piles of singles on one bobbin, each separated with a little piece of scrap fiber spun into the yarn if necessary. I then wind all of the singles off of the wheel bobbin onto three storage bobbins, breaking the yarn and beginning a new bobbin each time I finish a pile of singles or come to the scrap fiber insert. These singles can be plied, skeined, and washed in the same way I will treat larger skeins for the finished project to give me the most accurate sample possible.

The next step is to record how your sample was made. I use three-ring binders with note pages and half-pages with holes for storing yarn samples. I record information such as the date, where I purchased the fiber, what spinning wheel or spindle I used to create the sample, which drive ratio (pulley) I used for the singles and plying steps, and any other relevant comments. I wrap a length of singles around a card and paste it next to small samples of the unwashed and washed yarn. This is also a great place to make notes, draw sketches, and store fabric scraps and images that inspire your project. Our creative impulses are important—treat them with care and write them down. Keep them safe in your spinner's idea notebook, where they will wait for your return.

Pages from my spinning notebook.

What Can a Swatch Tell Us?

Swatches, or small samples that represent a larger textile, can tell us much, much more than stitches per inch or how colors will interact. Swatches can give us an idea about the durability, wear pattern, and drape of a textile before we invest much time in creating a finished piece. Working with multiple colors? A swatch is a great way to see if any of the yarns will bleed. After washing your swatch, pin it to a piece of foam, a cushion, or blocking mat. Leave the swatch to dry so it is somewhat vertical. Dyes that are mobile and not attached to the fiber surface will be more likely to move in the water column. Essentially, this test will promote bleeding if it is possible—good to know before proceeding with an entire piece. Another possibility is that the dye might fade in natural light. To test this, place your dry swatch in a sunny window for a few days with a piece of cardboard or a magazine covering half of the swatch. If the dyes are light sensitive, they will start to fade on the half of the swatch exposed to sunlight.

Winding a Center-Pull Ball by Hand

Part of my sampling and planning process is winding center-pull balls by hand. I love to feel the yarn passing through my fingers and think how a beautiful handspun yarn might be put to best use. You can use a tool called a *nøstepinne* to wind the same type of ball, but I enjoy tool-free winding.

The finished ball.

Simply lay the open skein across your knees and grasp the tail of yarn in your palm with your thumb pointing upward.

Wrap the yarn loosely a few times around your thumbnail in a clockwise direction.

Now, continue wrapping the yarn this way, but try to lay the wraps from the bottom right corner to the upper left corner of the yarn on your thumb. After laying a few wraps this way, rotate the ball clockwise a bit. Place a few more wraps and rotate clockwise again.

Continue wrapping and rotating being sure to keep the tail in your palm.

WORKING WITH WOOL:

Among the Birches Cowl

Handpainted tops are irresistible to many spinners. Commercial combed tops are made up of fibers that were straightened, aligned, and packed closely together to keep them orderly. These tidy, dense preparations provide dyers with a perfect palette to apply their color skills. Much like watercolor painting, the color effect produced on the fiber depends on how the dye is applied, how wet the fiber is during dyeing, and so on—it's quite an art in itself! Dyers can create a wide range of color effects from variegated solids, to muted transitions where the colors meet and merge, to sharp transitions, speckles, and splashes of color. Beyond the constant threat of colors blending too much and becoming "muddy" (but muddy can be quite nice, too), dyers also must handle the fibers carefully so they don't become felted.

A frequent lament of spinners is that these fibers, once spun into a two- or three-ply yarn, can look far different from the unspun fiber we fell in love with. The colors can change when mixed together during the plying process, giving a more speckled, blended appearance to the finished skein. Spinning these beautiful fibers in a way that retains the transitional colors takes extra consideration and can be a great challenge to the spinner.

While there are many ways we can handle and spin handpainted tops (such as chain plying), spinning fulled laceweight singles is one of my favorites. Fulling, or lightly felting, laceweight singles yarns can increase durability. The fulling process allows fibers to meet and begin to felt together a bit, and this process also eliminates some active twist. This means that we can spin a singles yarn with moderate twist, finish the skein, and end up with a strong yarn that will not twist stitches or finished fabric. These bouncy, lightweight yarns allow for slow color progressions, yielding finished pieces that look like the unspun handpainted top. This technique tends to be most effective with fine, crimpy, nonsuperwash wools and blends that are at least 50 percent wool.

This cowl is adapted from a shawl I designed for *Enchanted Knits* magazine. It is inspired by Huldra, an elf maiden who frequents the traditional folk tales of Norway. Huldra is one of the Hidden Folk, sometimes helpful, sometimes dangerous, who can appear suddenly in the forest.

This stitch pattern has strong horizontal and vertical movement, which is ideal for long color transitions. Knitting the pattern into a lace cowl is a great way to answer the perennial spinner's question, "What can I do with 4 ounces (113 g) of fiber?"

Sampling and Spinning

Because the fibers in combed top are very closely arranged and oriented parallel to the direction of spinning (off the end of the top), a worsted draw will usually work best. Another option is to spin from the fold, which will give the yarn a more muted effect. For the strongest color effect, fibers should stay as orderly and close together as possible. In fact, even predrafting or loosening the fibers can cause colors to mute. If the fibers are difficult to draft, try loosening them by snapping a length of top in the air like a whip a time or two, or gently loosen the fibers by spreading them apart (just a little bit!) perpendicular to the length of the top.

Fulled singles yarns can be easy to spin and require only one pass with a spinning wheel or spindle, but it is a good idea to spend time sampling first. How the gauge of the yarn, twist, and degree of fulling interact can yield very different results with small changes in drafting speed or number of cold-water rinses.

I have always adored the Laurelhurst colorway from Abstract Fiber. The mix of greens, from olive to chartreuse and moving into fuchsia, just makes my spinning fingers and water-colorist's eye very happy. This colorway is a great candidate for fulled singles because the unplied yarn will remain distinct and not become visually busy. I didn't split the top in any way because I wanted the color repeats to be as long as possible for the pattern that I chose. I also did not do any type of predrafting, which would have changed the placement of the color shifts, but I did loosen the fibers by gently opening the combed top

widthwise to reduce the compaction (not felting) that occurred when the fiber was dyed and packaged. I used the largest pulley on my Lendrum folding wheel (6:1 ratio) and spun a heavy laceweight singles using a short forward worsted draw.

Finishing

The Merino tops I chose seemed to felt with little help, so the fulling step was easy. I soaked the skeins in hot, soapy water to wash and fully wet the fibers. After 10 minutes or so, I squeezed the excess water out of the skeins and held them under a cold tap, turning them over to expose more of the surface to the running water before squeezing the excess water out. I returned the skeins to the hot water for a second wash and repeated this process two more times. After squeezing out the excess water once more, I gave each skein a few sharp snaps to realign the fibers. When drying singles yarns, I like to place a lightweight dowel through the bottoms of the hanging skeins to steady them during drying. The purpose is to keep the skeins hanging straight, not to weight or stretch them. I slip the skeins onto a hanging dowel and then place a second dowel through the bottoms of the skeins. If I used the same niddy-noddy to wind my skeins, they should all be the same length.

A variety of small samples combining different amounts of twist with different amounts of fulling.

Living with Wool

5

As handspinners, we are active stewards of textile history. From spinners who demonstrate at historical reenactments to spinners who push boundaries and definitions by creating decidedly modern yarns, we all take the skills we learn and interpret them into our own work. History and technique, just like fibers, are changed each time they pass through our hands. One of the best contributions we can make to our common history is to care for and keep records of the textiles we create and collect. It's important to remember that the textiles we create today can endure far beyond our lifetimes.

Record-Keeping

Handcrafted yarns and projects often have stories. Vibrant combed tops purchased on a special vacation, a special sheep's fleece transformed into a sheltering woven wrap, a handspun sweater knitted for a beloved friend—textiles carry the histories of their makers. These stories are important and if not recorded are easily lost.

Storage

Caring for your collection of woolen yarns and handmade textiles doesn't need to be complicated, but there are some factors to consider. Pests, light, and moisture can damage wool fibers in irrecoverable ways. Textiles created with intention and care deserve thoughtful storage.

Wool Moths

Pests vary regionally, but there are two common moths that can injure your wool stash. These small moths can cause quite a lot of damage and heartache if they are not discovered and removed as soon as possible. Clothes moths can be identified by what many people describe as a drunken flight pattern. They are weak flyers, so if you see one out and about, it is likely that there is an infestation hidden somewhere. They avoid light and so prefer undisturbed closets and corners. Moths that target your pantry (meal or grain moths) can be confused with clothes moths. One way to identify them is that when clothes moths land, their wings are held tightly against their bodies, making them similar in shape to a grain of rice.

Moths and Larvae

An important thing to remember is that the fluttering moths are often the most visible sign of a hidden infestation, but it is actually the larvae that damage textiles. And while they are drawn to protein-based fibers such as wool, alpaca, and angora, they will occasionally damage silk and even synthetics.

Webbing Clothes Moth
Tineola bisselliella

The adult moths lay eggs that look almost like grains of sand. These will often be near small, dark-colored granules of frass (excrement). When the eggs hatch, small, almost clear caterpillars will emerge. As they grow, they will become creamy white with dark heads. The adult moths are about a half inch long with tan or golden-colored bodies and russet heads.

Casemaking Clothes Moth
Tinea pellionella

The eggs of the casemaking moth will look the same as those of the webbing moth, but the larvae are a bit smaller. The larva shelters inside a silken case, sticking its head out of one end to eat. Because the case is often the color of what the larva is currently munching, it can be difficult to see. When the larva is hiding inside, the case will look almost like a noil in a ball of roving or a pill on a sweater. If you find what might be a case, pull the ends of the case apart to see if a larva is still active inside. The adult moths are a bit smaller than *Tineola bisselliella*, and they are brown with dark spots on the wings.

Webbing clothes moth.

Casemaking clothes moth.

Carpet beetles.

Carpet Beetles

There are a number of carpet beetle species, and while they are all quite small (about ⅛ inch [3 mm]), they can range from shiny black to intricate patterns of red, tan, and orange. The larvae range in color and shape; some are hairy and some are not. Often the first evidence of carpet beetles are skin casings that are shed by the larvae as they grow. These beetles are part of the environment and can move into homes fairly easily, traveling surprising distances. They earned their name when carpeting and rugs were more commonly made of wool, but they eat anything of animal origin. Carpet beetle infestations can be difficult to treat, and the best approach is to prevent an infestation from beginning. Just as a conservator would do in a museum collection, you should vacuum often, try to keep food and pets away from your stash as much as possible, and keep a watchful eye for insect damage.

Rodents

Bags of stored fleeces are a potential mouse palace—dark, quiet recesses and spaces, complete with handy bedding material, make a perfect place for mice and other small rodents to make nests and hide food stores. These small mammals can be trapped or poisoned, but if you live near pastures or large green spaces, this will be a losing battle. They play an important role in natural ecosystems, and the best strategy is to make your fiber storage area unappealing so they will do their important work elsewhere. Stuff steel wool into any crevices in your storage area that mice might enter, and keep bags of wool up off the floor to encourage air circulation.

Light

Avoid keeping fiber in direct sunlight over long periods of time. Wool isn't as easily damaged by ultraviolet rays as some fibers, such as silk, but direct long-term exposure will cause damage. Dyed and natural-color fibers can fade, sometimes quite quickly. Wool in plastic bags exposed to direct sunlight is especially at risk because condensation will form in the bag and damage the contents.

Moisture

If you have ever handled a fleece that was damp for long periods or a woolen jumper from the back of a musty closet, you will know that the odor is distinct. Damp or humid environments with a relative humidity over about 65 percent are prone to mold and can also inspire pests to set up residence. Not only are mold sources dangerous to human health, but textiles will also suffer if left untreated. If you live in a humid environment or an area with seasons of high humidity, check your fiber and woolen textiles on a regular basis.

Keeping Washed and Unwashed Fibers Separate

A handspinner's stash—a mix of unwashed wool, washed wool, yarns, and textiles—is particularly vulnerable to pests if stored together. The scent of raw wool can draw mice, moths, and carpet beetles and lead them straight to your handspun, handknitted sweaters. The climate where you live might make your stash more or less susceptible to certain pests, but good stash-keeping practices will keep your woolen items safe.

Bags, Bins, and Buckets

There are multiple storage strategies for wool. How you organize your stash will not only depend on what you are storing but also on the humidity in your environment and your storage areas.

Plastic Buckets with Lids

Early in my spinning life, I learned from Judith MacKenzie to keep raw and washed fleeces in plastic buckets with tightly fitting lids. As a wool classer, Judith saw that reducing air exposure in large wool bales could keep fleeces fresh for many years. Plastic buckets are an easy way to reproduce the effect of a wool bale in a size that will fit easily in a home storage space. Simply pack fibers into the bucket and make sure the lid fits tightly. I tape a label on the outside of the bucket to indicate the contents. Make sure that fleeces are fully dry before placing them in buckets.

Bags

Plastic bags are not recommended for long-term storage of textiles, especially in areas of high humidity or in storage spaces with temperature changes (such as attics) or direct sunlight. For long-term storage of clean fiber and textiles, use unbleached muslin bags rather than plastic. However, for nonarchival storage of fiber and yarn you want to access often, plastic bags can be handy. I use 2-gallon freezer bags for handspun yarns and fibers such as dyed locks and painted combed tops. In some cases, clothes moths can eat their way through plastic bags, so this is not an infallible method of storage when it comes to pests. However, clear bags are easy to monitor and may slow the spread of an infestation by segregating fibers within a stash.

Plastic Bins

Plastic bins are typically not airtight. Any small crevice around a handle or space between lid and bin will allow moths to enter, lay eggs, and create an infestation.

Baskets

While the sight of beautiful baskets brimming with washed locks can make a spinner's heart sing, it is a risky method of storage. I use small baskets for wool in my studio, but only for fibers that I am currently working with and that will not rest undisturbed for very long. I line these baskets with my favorite tea towels and check the bottom when I have emptied the basket. If there has been moth or carpet beetle activity, their frass (excrement) and possibly eggs will sift to the bottom of the basket and will be visible on the lining cloth. Wool moths are with us always—be ever vigilant!

Archival Storage

For special finished textiles or historical pieces that you have in your collection, archival-quality supplies provide the safest long-term storage. Acid-free boxes and tissue papers are readily available from online museum suppliers. There are also great resources available, such as *Preserving Textiles: A Guide for the Nonspecialist*, which explain how to properly store large items without creases, textiles with fringed edges, and damaged pieces.

Establish Quarantine Areas

As a new spinner, I bought some beautiful purple roving at a fiber festival, which I then put into a closet to save for a special project. Little did I suspect that I had also inadvertently brought home the makings of a moth infestation that would take me some time to eliminate. Since those grim days of ruthless purging of moth-tainted fibers, I have been careful to check and treat any new fiber coming into my studio. I've found moth eggs and larvae in fiber at festivals and shops, as well as in fiber I purchased online. I open shipments outside the house and put the fiber into plastic bags—keeping them isolated until I know they are clean. The shipping boxes, with many cracks and slots where eggs, larvae, and even adult moths and beetles can hide, never come into my home.

Unwashed wool can be stored for very long periods of time if it is tightly compressed and exposed to as little air as possible. But if you're like me, I have fleeces purchased from here and there that I intend to wash soon, but not the moment they arrive at my home. I have a quarantine area where I can keep raw fleeces, so they never darken my studio door until I know they are pest free.

Managing and Preventing Infestations

The types of insects or rodents likely to be a problem for you and your wool stash depend greatly on the environment in which you live. For most spinners, moths pose the greatest threat, and thoughtful storage and management can help. Moths are attracted to the scent of wool itself, and they find raw wool and textiles that are unwashed or have food stains particularly tasty. Many people use fragrances such as cedar or lavender to mask the scent of the wool. These natural aromatics can help to repel moths but do not kill them at any stage of their life cycle. Good housekeeping is one of the best ways to prevent infestations. Vacuum under cabinets and baskets, along baseboards, and in closets. Wash woolly sweaters, scarves, and hats before they are stored through the warmer parts of the year.

Even if you don't see adult moths flying, make a habit of visually inspecting your entire stash on a regular basis—at least twice a year, or more often if you can. Catching an infestation in the early stages can save a lot of hassle.

In some situations, pheromone traps can be a useful monitoring tool, especially if you have already found and treated an infestation and are unsure whether or not you have eliminated the problem. These small paper boxes contain a vial of pheromone to attract the adult moths, which are then trapped by the sticky surface inside the box. Keep in mind that traps are not a way to treat an infestation but are only used to indicate if moths are nearby. If you decide to try using traps, make sure to follow the manufacturer's instructions about spacing and placement. The pheromone lure will only attract moths within a limited range, so your traps will not give reliable information if they are spaced too far apart or located too far away from your stored wool. Some pheromones are capable of attracting multiple species of moths, not all of which are harmful to wool. Before you panic, make sure you have correctly identified anything caught in a trap. If you don't feel confident, inquire with a local pest-control specialist. Often they will help with identification for little or no charge.

Finding an infestation can bring tears to any spinner's eyes, but it is important to deal with the problem before it escalates. A dear friend of mine once suspected moths had invaded a few baskets of handspun. It was a busy time, and she didn't get to it right away. Months later, she was not only culling her moth-eaten yarns, but moth-infested furniture as well. There are a number of approaches for dealing with infestations, but none are foolproof. The best approach is to ruthlessly throw away any infested yarn or fiber. For textiles that are too special to be chucked or items that were near an infestation but don't show damage, the following methods can help to reduce the likelihood of reinfestation.

Temperature Treatments

Freezing is a common method of moth management, but it does have limitations. Freezing has a greater impact on larvae and adult moths than it does on eggs. Also, the temperature change needs to be as fast as possible to be effective. Research shows that exposure to -4°F (-20°C) for 15 hours will kill 99.99 percent of webbing clothes moths at all life stages. However, when wool is placed in the freezer, the fiber itself provides great insulation, and the temperature change in the interior of the wool can be slow enough that the insects can adapt to the cold unharmed.

Household freezers should be at least 0°F (-17°C), which will kill most larvae and adult moths, but this method is not as effective on eggs. As early as 1897, entomologists with the United States Department of Agriculture were finding that continuous cold (-8°C) was not an effective way to kill clothes moths and some species of carpet beetle, but allowing the item to warm before refreezing did eliminate the insects. Subsequent research has continued to fine-tune the process for museums and archives around the world. The reason that repeated exposure to temperature change works for clothes moths in particular is due to their life cycle. The eggs, which are least affected by cold, will hatch in about a week (in a warm room), but the larval stage, which is most affected by cold, can last anywhere from thirty-five days to two and a half years! If the first freeze takes care of the adult moths and larvae, and then a warming period allows the remaining eggs to hatch, those newly arrived larvae will likely be eliminated in the next freezer session.

To freeze wool or woolen textiles: Place the item to be treated in a plastic bag that closes tightly or wrap it in plastic sheeting and tape it shut, removing as much air as possible from the package; then put the item in the freezer. After about a week, take the package out of the freezer and allow it to sit at room temperature for another week. This will allow eggs that have not hatched to do so before you put it back into the freezer. When freezing treatments are complete, let the item warm to room temperature before opening the plastic bag; this will minimize condensation.

Heat can also be used to treat insect infestations but must be used with care. Wool that is placed in a plastic bag on a hot, sunny day will sweat and must be allowed to fully dry before re-storing.

Fumigating Fibers and Textiles

Another interesting treatment method used in museum collections is sometimes adapted for home use. This method involves placing the infested item in a modified atmosphere. Inert gases, such as carbon dioxide, can be used to displace oxygen and essentially suffocate insects. Many spinners treat infestations or suspected infestations by placing the item to be treated into a plastic bag with dry ice. Handling dry ice can be hazardous. For detailed instructions refer to the University of California's Integrated Pest Management website.

Insecticides can be used to fumigate woolen fibers and textiles. For proper handling, usage, and current options for approved chemicals, it is best to consult a pest-control specialist.

Glossary

ATTENUATE To draw fibers out under tension, such as in worsted-style spinning.

BATT A flat sheet of carded, ready-to-spin fibers typically prepared using a drumcarder.

BLOCKING A process in which the shape of a skein of yarn or finished textile has been slightly to dramatically altered. For handspun yarns, this often refers to a weight being added to skeins of yarn after washing.

BREAK A weak spot in a lock caused by a disturbance in a sheep's life—brief or prolonged illness, stress, or dietary change.

CARDING A fiber-preparation method in which fibers are opened and pulled more or less into alignment using a tool with many short teeth that are usually made of wire. Many different tools, large and small, hand or machine operated, can be used for carding, but the action is the same. A variety of fiber types and lengths can be mixed by the process. (See also Handcards)

CARDS (See Handcards)

CHAFF Small bits of hay or other vegetable matter that can collect in a fleece. This can be more difficult to remove in fine fleeces.

CLOUD Fibers that have been teased, picked, or carded into an unorganized mass of fibers are often called cloud. The locks may be loosened but still somewhat intact, or completely homogenous.

COMBED TOP A fiber preparation created using handcombs or an industrial combing process. Fibers are aligned and organized. Traditionally, the fibers would be longer than about 3 inches (7.5 cm) and all the same length.

COMBING A fiber-preparation process that separates long, prime fibers from waste, whether done by large industrial machines or using handcombs.

Combing can also be used to separate different types of fibers from the same fleece.

COMBS (See Handcombs)

CORESPUN YARN In this technique, prepared fibers (typically carded) are spun around the outside of a finished yarn, which serves as the core. The new fibers create a smooth or textured surface, often covering the core completely.

COTTING Felting of a fleece while still on the sheep.

CRIMP The natural wave and texture of a wool fiber. Crimp varies widely from one sheep breed to another.

CROSSBRED When sheep from two different breeds are mated, their offspring are described as crossbred. Many breeders choose to stick with purebred stock, but crossbreeding also introduces heterosis, or "hybrid vigor," into a flock.

CUTICLE Composed of overlapping rectangular scales that are arranged like shingles on a roof, the cuticle gives individual fibers a grain. Gently slide your fingers over the lock in each direction. The cuticle will feel smooth as your fingers move toward the tip of the lock and rougher as your fingers move toward the cut end.

DEHAIRING The process of separating the longer, coarser guard hairs from finer, shorter fibers within a fleece.

DIZ A small disk with at least one hole in the center used for drafting combed top. Most dizzes are also concave to act as a small funnel and direct the flow of fibers toward the orifice.

DRAFT The attenuation of fibers as they are prepared for spinning. Drafting can occur with or without the presence of twist.

DRAW A term often used for the many ways in which unspun fiber can be managed as the twist enters, creating yarn. (See also Long draw; Short draw)

DRUMCARDER Usually made up of two cylinders, or drums, wrapped in carding cloth. Fiber fed onto one drum is passed to another during rotation of the drums. Fibers build up in layers on the larger drum and form a batt, which can be removed and spun.

FINISHING A term that typically refers to washing but can include steaming or fulling. Handspun yarns for knitting, crochet, or embroidery are typically finished prior to use, while weaving yarns are usually finished as cloth. Fulling is a process in which wet skeins are handled more aggressively to begin the felting process.

FLICK CARDS or FLICKERS Often smaller than handcards, they are used to quickly tease individual locks of wool for spinning.

FULLING (See Finishing)

HAIR Guard hairs are long, coarse fibers that overlie finer, shorter fibers in some breeds of sheep and other fiber animals such as camels. These smooth fibers repel water, helping to protect the soft, insulating fibers growing closer to the animal's skin. Some sheep have heterotype hair, which can change as it grows through the seasons, shifting from smooth and coarse to thinner and more wool-like.

HANDCARDS Paddles covered with carding cloth made up of slightly bent wire teeth. Cards can be used to create a variety of preparations but are typically used to make rolags for woolen spinning.

HANDCOMBS Used to prepare combed tops for worsted spinning, combs have one to five rows (pitches) of long metal tines set into a wooden handle. Prime fiber is pulled off of the combs into a top, leaving waste behind.

KEMP Short, brittle fibers found in some fleeces. Undesirable in most breeds of sheep, but acceptable in some.

LANOLIN One of many compounds found in wool grease naturally produced by sheep. In practice, many people refer to the oily feel of raw wool as lanolin.

LAZY KATE (OR KATE) A device that holds bobbins filled with yarn while it is slowly fed into the spinning wheel during plying.

LOFT A term used by many handspinners to describe air space in yarns. Wools with strong crimp create loft, and increasing twist reduces loft.

LONG DRAW There are many variations on this style of spinning, but most involve the hand holding the unspun fiber moving away from the wheel an arm's length or so and then moving back toward the wheel's orifice as the yarn is fed onto the bobbin. The twist enters the drafting zone creating an airy yarn that is more fuzzy than smooth, typical of woolen yarns.

LUSTER The surface reflectance of a wool fiber, determined by the character of the fiber's cuticle.

MEMORY A term often used by textile workers and fiber artists for the resiliency of wool. Thanks to the structure and crimp of wool fibers, they are springy, returning to their natural shape if not stretched to the point of breakage. Memory will vary between wool types.

MOULT Considered a primitive characteristic, some sheep retain the ability to shed all or part of their fleece each year. This is the natural process of some healthy sheep, which is different from shedding of other types of sheep due to serious illness or stress. Other common terms are shed or rise.

NIDDY-NODDY A tool used to create a tidy loop, or skein, of yarn. Most are made so that the final skein will be of a known length, such as 1 or 2 yards. This allows the spinner to count the rotations and estimate yardage.

NOIL (NEP) A small tangle of fibers or group of short fibers in unspun fiber.

PICKER A device that teases locks open. Unlike in carding, fibers are not aligned in any way by picking.

PIN-DRAFTED ROVING Carded wool can be processed using a pin-drafting machine to further align the fibers. No short fibers are removed as in combing, but the pin-drafter attenuates the carded fibers, straightening them somewhat into a smoother, denser, more organized preparation for spinning.

PLY When two or more spun filaments are combined by spinning. For example, two singles that were spun to the right (Z-twist), can be made into a two-ply yarn by spinning them together to the left (S-twist).

PULLEY (See Whorl)

ROLAG A fiber preparation created using handcards. Wool is carded and then rolled into a tube so that the fibers are oriented perpendicular to the tube when spun from the end.

ROVING A spinning preparation typically created by a carding machine, but roving can also be created by hand. Fibers are somewhat parallel but are less organized than in a pin-drafted or combed preparation.

SCOUR To remove impurities from wool and textiles by washing.

SCURF Also referred to as skin flake or dander, scurf can range from a few tiny, dry flakes that fall out when the lock is teased to a more globular substance that can be a bit gummy and very difficult to remove. The term "scurf" is not common to all sheep and wool communities and is sometimes defined in other ways.

SECOND CUTS Short fibers that result from shearing. Motorized shears are flat and sheep are round so occasionally, the edge of the shearing blades will cut some locks midstaple. These are then shorn close to the skin, creating a "second cut."

SHED (See Moult)

SKEIN A yarn package with a continuous yarn wrapped into loops that are often 1 or 2 yards in circumference. The ends can be tied and the skein can be twisted into a tighter package for storage.

SKIRT To remove short or very dirty sections of wool from a fleece. This typically means removing the margins of the fleece, which is belly wool and wool that grew on the sheep's neck or down the legs.

SOUNDNESS Refers to a fleece without a break or other weakness. (See also Break)

STAPLE A distinct unit of fleece, also called a lock. Staple can also refer to the action of pulling locks from a fleece. To staple a fleece, locks are removed from the fleece individually and can then be washed, dyed, spun, etc.

SUINT Potassium-rich, water-soluble substance produced naturally by a sheep's skin. Often referred to as sheep sweat.

TAILSPUN YARN A textured yarn technique in which locks are spun into a continuous yarn with the tips of the locks hanging off the yarn like little tails. Before spinning, the locks are often carded lightly at the cut end only, allowing the rest of the lock to remain intact.

TEASE A term often used for pulling fibers out of lock formation. Loosening and opening fibers can make it easier to spin some types of yarns.

THRIFTY A term used by sheep producers for the types of animals that can grow and thrive with moderate nutrition and management.

TIPPY A nontechnical, common term used to describe a fleece that has had enough exposure to sun and rain to damage the outer tips of a fleece. As the tips of the fibers are damaged through environmental exposure, they often begin to stick together in little points at the end of each lock. This may or may not impact processing.

TOP (See Combed Top)

VEGETABLE MATTER (VM) Sheep that are not coated will pick up a bit (or a lot) of vegetation in their fleeces before shearing. Hay chaff, burrs and seeds from pastures, and straw bedding can contaminate a handspinning fleece.

WHORL Also called a pulley, it controls the ratio of speeds between the main drive wheel and flyer on a spinning wheel.

WOOL GREASE (See Wool Wax)

WOOLEN Like worsted, the term woolen can be applied to both fiber preparation and spinning style. A woolen preparation contains fibers that are fairly short and either disorganized or oriented perpendicular to the spinning direction, as in a carded rolag. (See Long Draw for more about woolen spinning)

WOOL WAX Natural oils produced by the sheep's skin, also called wool fat, lanolin, or yolk by spinners and wool workers. While these oily or waxy compounds are left in place by some handspinners until the yarn is spun, many spinners scour wool before spinning to remove impurities.

WORSTED Like woolen, the term worsted can be applied to both fiber preparation and spinning style. A worsted preparation contains fibers that are ordered and aligned parallel to the spinning direction, as in combed top. (See Short Draw for more about worsted spinning)

WORSTED DRAW A style of spinning in which the twist is prevented from entering the drafting zone. Either the forward hand pinches the point of twist and draws fibers forward, toward the orifice, or the fiber hand moves back, drafting the fibers. The forward hand then introduces twist into the newly drafted fibers.

YIELD The amount of clean wool that remains after shearing, skirting, and washing. Most often, yield will be expressed as the percentage of clean fleece recovered from a raw, unwashed fleece. This will vary for different fleece types and breeds.

YOLK A term used to describe a yellow stain that does not wash away. Additionally, yolk may refer to all that is washed away including grease and suint produced naturally by a sheep's skin as the wool grows.

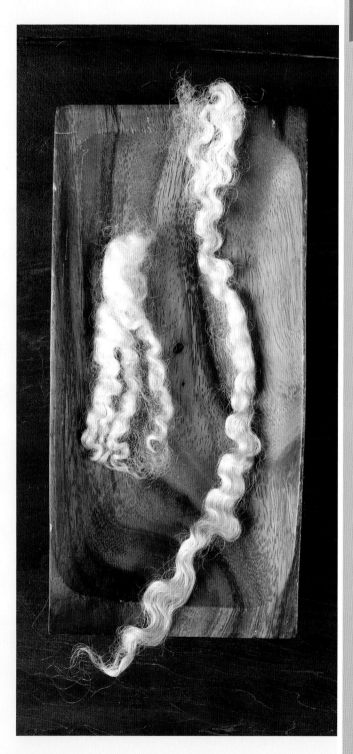

Further Reading

Amos, Alden. *The Alden Amos Big Book of Handspinning: Being a Compendium of Information, Advice, and Opinions on the Noble Art and Craft.* Fort Collins, Colorado: Interweave, 2001.

Anderson, Sarah. *The Spinner's Book of Yarn Design.* North Adams, Massachusetts: Storey Publishing, 2012.

Bates, Peter. *External Parasites of Small Ruminants, a Practical Guide to Their Prevention and Control.* Wallingford, Oxfordshire, England: CABI, 2012.

British Wool Marketing Board. *British Sheep and Wool.* Elliot, J., et al. ed. Bradford, England: British Wool Marketing Board, 1990.

Burnley, James. *The History of Wool and Woolcombing.* London: Low, Marston, Searle and Rivington, 1889.

Casey, Maggie. *Start Spinning: Everything You Need to Know to Make Great Yarn.* Fort Collins, Colorado: Interweave, 2008.

Field, Anne. *Spinning Wool: Beyond the Basics.* Rev. ed. North Pomfret, Vermont: Trafalgar Square Books, 2010.

Fournier, Nola, and Jane Fournier. *In Sheep's Clothing: A Handspinner's Guide to Wool.* Fort Collins, Colorado: Interweave, 1995.

Fossnes, Heidi. *Håndplagg til Bunader og Folkedrakter.* Oslo: Damm, 2012.

Franquemont, Abby. *Respect the Spindle.* Fort Collins, Colorado: Interweave, 2009.

Gravjord, Ingebørg. *Votten I Norsk Tradisjon.* Oslo: Landbruksforlaget, 1986.

Hartsuch, Bruce E. *Introduction to Textile Chemistry.* New York: John Wiley & Sons, Inc., 1950.

Hoffmann, Marta. *Frå Fiber til Tøy.* Oslo: Landbruksforlaget, 1991.

James, J. *History of the Worsted Manufacture in England, From the Earliest Times.* London: Longman, Brown, Green, Longmans, and Roberts; and Charles Standfield, Bradford, 1857.

Kahn, Cynthia M. *The Merck Veterinary Manual.* Revised/Expanded ed. Whitehouse Station, New Jersey: Merck, 2010.

Klos, Dagmar. *Dyer's Companion.* Fort Collins, Colorado: Interweave, 2005.

Laurenson, Sarah. ed. *Shetland Textiles: 800 BC to the Present.* Lerwick, Scotland: Shetland Heritage Publications, 2013.

Lupton, C. J., D. F. Waldron, and F. A. Pfeiffer. "Prickle Factor in Fleeces in Performance-tested Fine-wool Rams." *Sheep & Goat Research Journal Vol. 17, no. 1* (2001).

MacKenzie, Judith. *The Intentional Spinner.* Fort Collins, Colorado: Interweave, 2009.

Mailand, Harold F. and Dorothy Stites Alig. *Preserving Textiles: A Guide for the Nonspecialist.* Indianapolis, Indiana: The Indianapolis Museum of Art, 1999.

Menz, Deb. *Color in Spinning.* Fort Collins, Colorado: Interweave, 2005.

Østergård, Else. *Woven into the Earth: Textiles from Norse Greenland.* Aarhus, Denmark: Aarhus University Press, 2009.

Rare Breeds Survival Trust. rbst.org.uk.

Robson, Deb and Carol Ekarius. *The Fleece and Fiber Sourcebook.* North Adams, Massachusetts: Storey Publishing, 2011.

Ryder, M.L. *Sheep and Man.* London: Duckworth, 1983.

Ryder, M. L. and S. K. Stephenson. *Wool Growth.* London: Academic Press, 1968.

Simpson, W.S., and G.H. Cranshaw, eds. *Wool: Science and Technology.* Cambridge, England: Woodhead

Publishing Limited in association with The Textile Institute, 2002.

Strang, Thomas J. "A Review of Published Temperatures for the Control of Pest Insects in Museums." Collections Forum 8: 41–67.

Stove, Margaret. *Merino: Handspinning, Dyeing, and Working with Merino and Superfine Wools.* Fort Collins, Colorado: Interweave, 1991.

Stringleman, Hugh and Robert Peden. "Sheep Farming—Importance of the Sheep Industry." *Te Ara: The Encyclopedia of New Zealand*; TeAra.govt.nz.

The Livestock Conservancy (Formerly the American Livestock Breeds Conservancy); livestockconservancy.org

Thomas, J. F. H. *Sheep*. London: Faber & Faber, 1945.

Teal, Peter. *Hand Woolcombing and Spinning: A Guide to Worsteds from the Spinning-wheel*. Revised/Expanded ed. Poole, England: Blandford Press, 2005.

Photo Credits

Paulette and Chip Brown/Fiddlehead Hollow: p. 16; Clemson University, USDA Cooperative Extension Slide Series, Bugwood.org: p. 147 (left and center); Joe Coca: pp. 94–95; Whitney Cranshaw, Colorado State University, Bugwood.org: p. 147 (right); Kim Day/Red Rope Farm: p. 39 (bottom); Sally Fox/Viriditas Farm: p. 47; Sonia and Alan Glover/Windy Ridge Flock: p. 26 (bottom); Kate Larson: pp. 4, 21, 28 (left), 36 (top), 49, 56, 93, 107–108; Little Smoky Blues: p. 29; Yvonne and Doug Madsen/Spinners Eden Farm: pp. 13, 44 (bottom); Vesterheim Norwegian-American Museum, Decorah, Iowa: pp. 70, 112 (right)

Fiber Directory

For more breed-specific fiber sources, contact the shepherds and fiber artists listed in the breed section beginning on page 17.

Abstract Fiber
abstractfiber.com
Handpainted yarn and fiber

Ashland Bay
ashlandbay.com
Combed tops in a wide range of fibers

Crosspatch Creations
spinningfiber.net
Fleece and batts

Frabjous Fibers
frabjousfibers.com
Hand-dyed fibers

Handspun by Stefania
stefania-spins.com
Roving and hand-spun yarns dyed with natural materials

Jamieson and Smith, Shetland Woolbrokers, Ltd.
shetlandwoolbrokers.co.uk
Shetland yarns and combed tops

LunabudKnits
lunabudknits.com
Hand-dyed yarns and fibers, handspun yarns, smooth and textured batts

Louet North America
louet.com
Roving and combed tops

New England Felting Supply
feltingsupply.com
Norwegian wool batts and Pelsull locks

Solitude Wool
solitudewool.com
Breed-specific yarns and fibers

Sweetgrass Farm
sweetgrass-jacobs.com
Jacob fleeces and roving

Zeilinger Wool Company
zwool.com
Fiber-processing services

Index

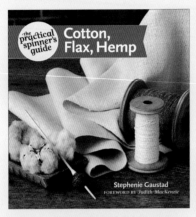